The Garden of Good and Evil Pancakes

David S. Atkinson

Advanced Praise for David S Atkinson's The Garden of Good and Evil Pancakes

David S. Atkinson grasps the "secret" of striking fiction (or should I say, nightmares?), he knows you've got "to find some place where the facts didn't shout so loud," and in this unnerving Garden (or should I say, inferno?), he's found a place full of whispers (or should I say, moans?). These insidious pieces develop like an advent calendar on which the surface seems drab yet unsettled, the stuff of Raymond Carver, and yet behind each door hide the eyepopping, amoral fairy-folk of Henry Darger. Don't wait till December to start.

--John Domini
author of The Sea-God's Herb

The Garden of Good and Evil Pancakes is a modern-day Waiting for Godot set in a diner, only with more engaging dialogue and fully-realized characters. At times Atkinson will have you asking what you want for dinner. But by the end, you'll be asking what you want for (and from) life. A brilliant achievement of existentialism without the pretension.

--Nathaniel Tower
author of Nagging Wives, Foolish Husbands and Managing Editor of Bartleby Snopes Literary Magazine and Press

Hell is other people and pancakes. Or to be more accurate, purgatory is other people and pancakes--and friendships and heartaches and the dull, deceiving comfort of things staying exactly the same. Be careful what you wish for in David S. Atkinson's funny, flippant book - you just might get it, along with endless coffee refills and a lifetime of breakfast food.

**-- Amber Sparks
author of May We Shed These Human Bodies**

Reading David Atkinson's The Garden of Good and Evil Pancakes instills the same sort of hunger that got me into literary fiction in the first place. It brings with it humor and honesty while managing to be clever and sickly sweet. That savory combination isn't found very often. Buy the book and dive in with a short stack drenched in maple syrup.

**-- Michael J Seidlinger
author of The Laughter of Strangers**

My vision of hell involves being trapped in a Wal-Mart, but in The Garden of Good and Evil Pancakes, David S. Atkinson makes a good case for Village Inn. On the other hand, he argues that it could be heaven: drinks are refilled, breakfast is always served, and the check never arrives. What more could you want? Filled with a cast of characters brought to life through the vivid imagination of Cassandra, lovers of literary fiction will enjoy this wildly inventive story. I know I did!

**--Jeremy Morong
author of On the Backs of Dragons**

The Garden of Good and Evil Pancakes

This is a work of fiction. All the characters and events portrayed in this book are fictitious, and any resemblance to real people or events is purely coincidental.

Copyright © 2014 and 2018 by David S. Atkinson

All rights reserved, including the right to reproduce this book, or portions thereof, in any form.

Cover Illustration by Brian Forrest

ISBN: 978-1-942856-32-0

Literary Wanderlust | Denver, Colorado

*To Joseph Michael Owens
and
Donald Antrim*

David S. Atkinson

is the author of Bones Buried in the Dirt, The Garden of Good and Evil Pancakes, Apocalypse All The Time, and Not Quite So Stories.

His short fiction has appeared in Bartleby Snopes, Grey Sparrow Journal, Interrobang?! Magazine, Atticus Review, Sundog Lit, Midnight Circus, and others.

His book reviews have appeared in American Book Review, The Rumpus, [Pank], The Lit Pub, HTML GIANT, and others.

His writing website is www.davidsatkinsonwriting.com and he spends his non-literary time working as a patent attorney in Denver.

He eats at Village Inn as often as once a week and frequently enjoys the multigrain pancakes.

Acknowledgements

First thanks have to go to Joseph Michael Owens and Donald Antrim. Donald Antrim wrote The Verificationist and Joseph Michael Owens recommended it to me. I got a weird idea what The Verificationist was going to be that turned out totally wrong. I told Joe as I was reading and loving what I had expected and he replied: "You should write that." This book is what came from listening to Joe's good advice.

I also want to thank the whole crew over at EAB Publishing. Tim Benson, AE Stueve, Julie Rowse, Britt Sullivan, and anyone else involved I wasn't personally fortunate enough to know by name yet. They took a look at my novel, decided to publish it, and went through an incredible amount of work in editing, marketing, and a slew of other things I'm probably not even aware of. If I wore a hat, it would be off to them. There would be no book without all of them.

Thanks also to Brian Forrest, the artist responsible for the cover. I'm sure you'll agree, he does amazing work.

The Garden of Good and Evil Pancakes

David S. Atkinson

SUNDAY

Breakfast

"Here's something for you," I told Thomas and Kate. We needed something to pass the time since it wasn't moving on its own. I was looking over a menu, but none of us were hungry right then. Dirty dishes were already all over the table of our Village Inn booth. "Describe a breakfast item as someone suffering in purgatory. Think Dante."

"Any item?" Thomas asked, leaning in but keeping his hand on Kate's leg under the table. They were snuggled together on their side of the booth. I was by myself on mine.

Kate leaned back in the booth, crossing her arms over her blood red camisole top. She turned her head, causing her long white-blond ponytail, tied closely to her scalp, to flick at Thomas. Not in an aggressive way, maybe more as some kind of reminder.

"Doesn't matter," I said. "It's more of a challenge to just pick one without thinking about it beforehand. Improv it. See what you come up with on the spot."

"Maybe you should just assign us one, Cassandra," Thomas suggested. He tried to swish his now short-clipped, dirty-brown hair, obviously still used to when it was long. It was a bowl cut, the hairstyle for someone who doesn't grasp respectable haircuts but suddenly has to have one.

"I've got one," Kate snapped, sitting forward but leaving her arms crossed. "Steak and eggs."

I was the only one looking at a menu, but steak and eggs was on there in some fashion. It wasn't like we didn't know the menu by heart at that point anyway, but the exact titles didn't matter. We'd earned the right to refer to things by generalities. I didn't bother checking whether this one was a title or a gist. I let it slide.

"Okay," I replied, adjusting to pull up my grey Nike sweat suit bottoms. "Steak and eggs. Go."

"Steak and eggs," Kate repeated, straightening up more.

Thomas turned toward her to listen and I set the menu down on the table.

"It's really the eggs," she explained, "not the whole combo. The eggs are the reason both the eggs and steak are in purgatory. The steak didn't do anything wrong but is there anyway."

"Does that count?" Thomas asked. "Since it isn't the whole meal?"

He looked hopeful, like he didn't want me to challenge her on it but worried I might. I shrugged. "Her choice. I'll let it go if she's got a good story for it."

Kate nodded. "Right, the whole point is that they don't go together. They're two separate things that only travel together because of common custom. Really, each is totally on its own as far as an actual meal goes. They don't add up to anything."

"So where's the tension?" I prompted. I couldn't resist doing at least that much.

"It's the eggs." She glared at me. "The eggs could never accept that her and the steak weren't a package deal. They need to separate, let the steak move on, but the eggs can't do that."

"Like a drowning swimmer," Thomas chimed in. "The lifeguard is there to try to save, but the swimmer mucks it up by panicking and climbing all over everything. All the swimmer has to do is relax and the lifeguard could save them both, but the swimmer can't let go."

"Sort of," Kate continued. "The steak really belongs at dinner, not breakfast at all. It has ambitions and capabilities, something bigger to be. The steak feels guilty, though, since it got its early start with the eggs. The eggs need to let the steak loose so it can develop and mature, but the eggs can't see as far as dinner because eggs have no place there."

"That's depressing," Thomas commented.

She turned to him. "She did say purgatory."

"It's true," I conceded. "If it was completely pleasant then there'd be no suffering, no reason for purgatory."

"Thank you," Kate said, turning back to me. "That's why the eggs are in purgatory. If the eggs could let go then they could both leave. The eggs can't grasp that, though, so they're both stuck."

"And what do the eggs get to do if the steak moves on to dinner?" I asked, playing along. "What's the motivation to let go if there is no hope of ever attaining dinner?"

"They get eaten." Kate smiled, showing an almost predatory amount of teeth. "It's what would have happened anyway, but at least the eggs won't be stuck anymore. They would be their own breakfast and finally be at peace."

An uncomfortable blanket of silence fell over the booth. Thomas looked back and forth at each of us, like he was hoping one of us was about to talk. I sipped at my coffee.

"Let me do one," Thomas finally said, reaching for the menu. "See if I can't come up with something a little more upbeat."

"Remember," I warned him, "this is purgatory. It can't be too happy."

He nodded, scanning the breakfast section of the menu. I don't know why he did that. Maybe it lent some kind of textual authority to what he was about to say. Both Kate and I knew he didn't need to read anything to pick an item.

"Eggs Benedict," he announced.

"Very bold," Kate replied. "I wonder why eggs Benedict might be in purgatory."

"It has a certain charm," I offered. "The only breakfast not commonly served with pancakes. It's unique, truly a self-contained breakfast."

"That's it." Thomas nodded. "Eggs Benedict only ever wanted to be a united breakfast. It's all there, English muffin, ham, poached egg, and hollandaise. Tastiest of the breakfasts. Truly perfect. It's attained everything it ever wanted to be, everything it ever could be. Eggs Benedict should be truly happy."

"So why is it in purgatory?" I challenged. I looked at Kate and she nodded sharply, as if seconding the challenge.

"Easy." He smiled. "It's there because of its name. For some reason, people got the idea it was a traitor just because of the Benedict thing. I don't know, maybe they got jealous because eggs Benedict could be that happy. Either way, it's branded, carrying the stigma of a traitor."

"So God doesn't know it's really innocent?" Kate asked. "Seems a bit weak to me."

"No," Thomas countered, "it isn't in purgatory because people think it's a traitor; it's there because of its own self-loathing over the fact that people think it."

Kate pursed her lips and nodded thoughtfully, apparently starting to go along with Thomas's logic. I had to admit it. Even I found it persuasive.

"All it had to do was be happy about being perfect, but it let the rumors get to it. Maybe it even believed it was a traitor somehow despite the fact that it hadn't done anything. The eggs Benedict blames itself for what other people thought about it and can't see that it's just other people talking."

"And so it's stuck," I concluded. "It can't move on until it realizes it never did anything wrong. It's trapped until it ignores what other people think."

"Yup." Thomas grinned. "That's about the size of it. Not bad, eh?"

"I don't think that's any less depressing than mine," Kate commented, "but it works."

I drained my coffee. Looking at the empty cup, I grabbed the portable pot the waitress had left at the table. Then it was full again, as if I hadn't drunk it to begin with. Its previous state, unchanged . . . similar to how so many other changes were erased at the Village Inn.

"Well?" Thomas prompted.

"Well what?"

"It's your turn," he reminded. "You've got to come up with one. We both did it."

I looked at them. "You want me to?" Kate shrugged and Thomas nodded. "All right, the garden skillet."

"Personally," Kate chimed in, "I think the garden skillet has a lot it needs to be forgiven for. I'm not sure purgatory is a bad enough place for it. Seems like someplace worse might be more appropriate."

"Exactly," I agreed, even though I really didn't.

"I don't know," Thomas tried to counter. "It's healthy, low-fat. That doesn't seem completely wrong."

"But it's way too vain," I explained. "It thought that it was fine on its own, but it needed a few less vegetables and definitely needed ham chunks instead of relying on being served with a side of bacon. It was born to be the Denver skillet, but it never knew it."

"And it's in purgatory for just that?" Thomas asked.

"It is," I insisted. "It has to stay there because it's not complete and it can't ever be complete without ham chunks. There's no other way. Once it gets ham chunks, then it can go on to the heavenly hereafter."

"But then it wouldn't be the garden skillet anymore," Kate interjected.

I nodded. "That's true, but the garden skillet has to change into another form if it ever wants to leave purgatory. That's just the way it is."

Thomas looked out the window to avoid responding, peeking through the half-closed blinds of our booth. Kate looked over at him.

"That one kind of stinks," Kate said. "I think one of us wins that game."

"It isn't about winning," I countered, "it's about purgatory. And breakfast."

I should probably mention that we must have been in that Village Inn for at least several years by that point. This whole thing probably makes a bit more sense if I do. We didn't seem to be able to leave and the waitress just kept serving us, even though it wasn't a 24 hour restaurant. Nobody else in the restaurant seemed to notice, so we just kept passing the time.

Lunch

I realized I had been spaced out for a while, staring at the reflection of my black hair in the lid of the pepper shaker. My first instinct was to snap myself out of it, but I remembered that there was no real need to do so. We were still stuck at the Village Inn; that probably wasn't going to change anytime soon.

And, after all, I had good hair. I might not have been a Nordic ice princess like Miss Long and Blond across the table, but not many women could pull off a pixie cut in their early 20s. Even fewer looked good doing it. I did both. I'd never asked Thomas which he preferred, but he'd never complained while we were together.

Thomas was stacking non-dairy creamers when I finally decided to quit checking out my hair. He probably had been doing that for a while from the look of the little structure being constructed on the table.

From the size of whatever it was, I'm guessing it was a little bridge, he must have collected all the non-dairy creamers on the table. Little plastic buckets with the paper caps on top. Just peel off and use. They're probably supposed to look like some old-style milk pail and evoke thoughts of fresh dairy, but nobody alive remembers those and we just recognize them as the familiar non-dairy creamers.

"This means something," Thomas mumbled facetiously, still building, even though it didn't.

Whatever he was building had a base on two sides and met over the middle. All from stacking little creamers. From there he stacked more on top of the middle part. It looked like some kind of bridge.

"Excuse me," Kate called to a waitress passing by to drop syrup off at another table. She wasn't even our waitress. "Could we get a few more creamers over here?"

The waitress should have said no. I certainly would have. I was the only one drinking coffee at the table, maybe that's why Kate and Thomas slept in the booth sometimes and I never did, and I drank it black. We weren't even really using the non-dairy creamers we already had. It just cluttered the table to bring more.

"Here you are," the waitress said a few minutes later, roughly dumping a couple bowls of the things on the table. Clearly she knew what we were doing with them. She must have not cared since it wasn't her table.

"Thanks," Kate replied, smiling wide, though so much that it ended up twisting into a bit of a sneer. "Here." She turned and presented them to Thomas as if she'd gotten them herself. "Now you can make it bigger."

"Fair enough," Thomas agreed and started taking his bridge down in order to rebuild it over again.

So, Kate was going to help him with the little toy. "Wait," I ordered. "I'll be right back."

If we were going to get serious about building that bridge, we were going to need a lot more creamers than that. A few supplemental bowls just wasn't thinking big enough. It was a good idea, I gave Kate that much, but she needed to be a little more creative if she was going to be on the bridge crew. I figured I could do better.

Pretending to wander around the tables on the way to the bathroom, which was right near our booth, I started sneaking creamers from empty tables that hadn't been cleared yet. I was sneaky at first, but I became bolder when no one appeared to care. I even asked a few occupied tables if I could have theirs. Most didn't question and just handed them over. It was only right, since they weren't going to be there for anywhere near as long as we apparently were.

"Here," I said after I finally decided I had enough, dumping my haul all over the table. They knocked over the restarted bridge. "Now this should be enough."

Really, I'd stopped gathering because I couldn't carry any more. Also, I didn't want Thomas to finish before I got back and not need what I'd gathered. Either way, they didn't need to know that.

"Too much is always enough," Kate commented.

"Okay then," Thomas concluded, apparently ignoring her. "Here we go again."

He cleared a larger space on the table and started building the two bases up again. This time he spread them out a bit wider, since we were going to build it quite a bit bigger. It was the same design, though, just on a bigger scale.

Kate and I started helping, adding creamers to the stacks. She was doing it wrong, though, stacking each layer upright so the bottom of one rested on the paper lids of the layer below.

"You've got to switch them off," I said, turning a creamer upside down to demonstrate. "Stack them so paper touches paper and plastic bottoms touch bottoms. That's more stable."

It was, too. The paper lids bulged out a little from the nondairy creamer inside. I don't know why they put so much in each, causing the bulges, but that was the situation we found ourselves in. Maybe it gave people a sense of value, bulging like that. Still, stacking the narrower bases on the bulge made them tip. Bulge to bulge worked better because the tops were wider than the bases.

"But it's uglier that way," Kate argued, still stacking as she had been. "Aesthetics are important as well, and it's not that much less stable. You should switch so it doesn't look like crap so much."

She was kind of right about that, I realized. I wondered if I could poke each with a pin and let out the excess. They'd stack better that way, but I didn't have a pin. I didn't relish the monotony of that particular task either.

"Stability is more important than looks," I shot back, "and it doesn't look that much prettier your way. Not enough to justify the sacrifice to function. Besides, doing both looks worse than either."

"All the more reason to do things my way." She smirked.

I looked at Thomas, but he wasn't even paying attention. He was absorbed in stacking; no concern at all for the architectural disagreement that threatened the literal foundations of his trivial little creation.

"Well," I snapped back before thinking of a good retort, forcing me to say the next thing I would think of regardless of what it was, "aesthetics are secondary considerations when building a bridge. Stability must be primary. Any stability sacrifice is akin to a crime for a bridge, no matter how pretty or ugly the results."

"Bridge?" Kate wrinkled her tiny little nose. Thomas looked up from his work, looking confused. "It's a skyscraper, not some dumb bridge."

"Of course it's a bridge," I insisted. "Look at how that bit in the middle stretches over nothing to bring the two different bases together. What else is it if it goes over something?"

Kate sniffed. "Looks like a skyscraper to me. It just has an open courtyard underneath the main tower so people can walk around. The two supports just hold up the main tower so it can have that without crashing."

Thomas looked down at the structure, a non-dairy creamer he'd been about to place still in his hand. Kate and I both looked at him. The booth was silent.

"I hadn't really thought of it as anything," Thomas said. "I guess I didn't care what it was. I was just building. I suppose it can be a skyscraper, though," he continued after glancing at Kate. "If I had to pick."

Needless to say, I was pretty sick of creamer buildings by that point. Absent any other choice, though, we kept building the 'skyscraper.'

Dinner

I was lying back on my side of the booth, my head down on the seat and my legs draped over the end. Someone at normal height wouldn't have seen me, unless they were standing right next to the table.

It wasn't that I was sleepy. As I mentioned before, I hadn't slept since we'd gotten to the Village Inn. I don't know why. I just never seemed to need to sleep, or want to. At that particular moment I was just bored, sick of sitting up for so long.

Kate and Thomas were playing cards. They had been for some time, though I'm not sure where they'd gotten the Tropicana casino themed cards. Maybe they'd brought them with when we first arrived. I didn't really care so I didn't think about it much. I wasn't even sure what game they were playing. It sounded like hearts.

"Hey," I said, sitting up so I could see them. "Something just occurred to me."

"That pancakes can't really be cakes if we don't frost them?" Thomas asked, playing a three of clubs.

I couldn't tell whether he was serious or not. "Of course not. Don't be ridiculous."

"What then?" Kate asked, setting a seven of hearts on the table.

"Village Inn," I said, "is modeled on corporate America's boardroom conception of what heaven is like. Or, at least what we think we imagine heaven to be."

Thomas looked around, eyes narrowing and widening as he scanned the patrons and booths in turn as if seriously considering the proposition. Kate, on the other hand, drew another card. "I don't see it," she said.

"Think about it. You work and slave unquestioningly all your life to get money. Once you do get money, or at least a certain amount, you can come here to trade in all that accumulated merit for your saturated-fat breakfast reward."

"Heaven's reward is pancakes?" Thomas asked. Apparently he was a bit fixated on pancakes at that particular moment.

"There had better be more to this argument than that," Kate warned, rearranging the cards in her hand.

"No," Thomas countered, "I think I see where she's going with this. See how cloudlike and bland it is in here? Peaceful? It's blue and orange instead of white and gold, but still. There might as well be people floating by strumming harps. Faceless people, of course."

"Right." I nodded. "And people who come here don't have to toil anymore. At least, as long as their money holds out. Someone else does everything. Cooking, cleaning, servicing, seating, everything is taken care of."

"Chewing," Kate mentioned.

"True, there's still that, but that's part of the heaven of it. Satisfaction of desire. If someone else chewed for you then you might as well be in limbo. You still have to go through the effort of enjoying."

"I might as well be in limbo," Kate muttered.

"It's got the earmarks of heaven," Thomas conceded, "other than the charging part."

"It is supposed to be the corporate idea of heaven," I insisted. "Besides, no one's brought us a bill yet. For the moment, it might as well all be free."

"All right," Kate interrupted, "how's this: we aren't dead. Absent some kind of Rod Serling thing where we died and don't know, we therefore can't be in heaven."

"Wait," Thomas said, "weren't there biblical prophets who were taken to heaven bodily? I swear I remember something about that. Maybe that could have happened to us while we weren't paying attention."

"Elijah, Enoch, maybe a few others," I replied. "Anyway, it doesn't matter. I didn't say we were in heaven, just that Village Inn is modeled on a particular vision of heaven."

"I'm glad you don't think I'm dead," Kate replied.

"But think about it," I continued, "the food makes a lot more sense if you were acting like there wouldn't be any consequences anymore. Pancakes, sausage, eggs, all that is heavenly delicious but loaded with calories and fat. In heaven, however, you'd be free to enjoy yourself without having to worry. There'd be no heart attacks or diabetic comas waiting to happen, or stretch pants that won't fit."

I honestly didn't intend that last bit as an attack on the black skinny jeans Kate was wearing. She grimaced when I said it, though. How could she take that wrong? Skinny jeans are the exact fashion opposite of fat person stretch pants. Even I admit that much.

"You'd be free to pig out as much as you wanted," I continued.

Thomas looked down at his cards. Kate took a sip of water and pushed an empty plate further from her. I waited, hoping they'd get over it and get back to my discussion. Silence reigned at the booth.

"How about the fact that the food is good, but isn't exactly fine dining?" Thomas finally asked, looking over at Kate. "Shouldn't the food in heaven be a little more impressive? Something chef-inspired?"

Kate nodded her head strongly.

"Okay, good point," I admitted. "But . . . that goes back to the 'bland' thing you mentioned earlier. It's trying to be heaven to a large cross-section of lower to middle class America at the same time. Let's call it non-objectionable heaven. They can't risk alienating people with food they don't understand and can't appreciate."

"So, instead of beef wellington you get comfort food?"

"Sure," I agreed. "It's got sugar. It's got fat. Everybody likes it, whether they admit it or not, but it's got nothing that's going to ruffle anybody's feathers. Nothing distracting. Remember, flash and dazzle are the tools of the devil. The Lord needs no such ornamentation."

"Okay," Kate conceded, sitting up straighter and putting her cards face down on the table. "But what about the fact that they don't discriminate at the door? Don't only the holy get into heaven?"

I thought about that. "Well, corporate America is still primarily motivated by profit. I suppose they had to fudge on the judging people part a little bit."

"A little? Anyone who walks in gets a table!"

"Ah ha," Thomas interrupted. "No shirts, no shoes, no service. There are minimum standards for heaven."

"True." Kate nodded quickly at Thomas before turning back to me. "Still, beyond that, anyone can get served here. Murderers, rapists, anybody. They'll seat you as long as they have an open table. It's based on their merits, not yours."

I reluctantly nodded. I hated when she had a point, even when I didn't care about winning. "You do have to have money, though. That's the ultimate corporate merit: spending power."

"Not necessarily." She shook her head. "You might have stolen the money, maybe even from them. There's no corporate idea of goodness in that. Besides, they don't even know whether you have money or not until it's time to pay. Until then, it's anybody's guess."

I had nothing to say to that, unfortunately. Instead, I just shrugged my shoulders and waited for her to continue. Thomas sat there like a patient little puppy dog.

"It's all reward, but possibly for no deserving act. That isn't a reward at all, or heaven for that matter. It's a gift."

"But a gift that costs money," I clarified. "At least, in theory it does."

"Right," Kate agreed, nodding. Finally.

Kate picked up her cards and shuffled them around in her hand. She and Thomas continued playing their game. I still couldn't tell what they were playing.

I got up and went to the bathroom. I didn't even have to go; I just went. I did that sometimes. Just sat in there. I guess it broke up the monotony. It's not like Kate or Thomas would know unless I told them. Even when Kate and I went to the bathroom at the same time, we obviously used different stalls so she didn't know what I was doing. It was my little secret alone time.

"Another thing," Kate snapped when I sat down again, "all there is to do here is eating. There's nothing else."

"Okay," I replied. "I never said there was. Regardless, consumption is the cornerstone of corporate American theology. It makes sense that it would be the foundation for their idea of heaven."

"But it's boring! It's mind-numbingly boring," she protested.

"I've got no disagreement with that," Thomas mumbled.

Really, I didn't either. We were bored. We could order whatever we wanted, without any apparent consequences of any kind, but also had no reason at all to do so. Currently, we were at best hoping to become hungry again so we wanted to order something else.

"I just can't enjoy doing nothing," Kate continued. "Eating is basically nothing. There's no advancement, no improvement. There's nothing to do and no reason to do it. How can that possibly be heaven?"

"But you can't improve in heaven," Thomas reminded. "It's over by then. Heaven is the end, hopefully. Eternity. There's no more struggle, no more strife."

"I know," she replied, "but I just can't be happy thoughtlessly chewing like a cow all day. There's just no way. Could you? Honestly? Wouldn't you need something more?"

Thomas took a drink of his Coke. "I suppose, when it really comes down to it."

I decided to stay silent. Currently the idea of doing nothing seemed pretty boring, but maybe it wouldn't be boring in actual heaven. In some way, it still sounded kind of good.

"I just have to think there'd be something more to do in heaven," Kate told Thomas. "I don't know what it would be, but it would have to be something more than just eating."

Thomas nodded sweetly at her. She grabbed his hand and squeezed. I tasted bile in the back of my mouth, but maybe that was one of the many things I'd eaten.

"Anyway," she said to me, looking around the Village Inn, "this just doesn't seem much like my idea of heaven. I guess that's all I'm saying."

"Mine either," I replied.

Sides

There was no real way to tell how long we'd been stuck inside the Village Inn. None of us had watches or phones. It kept getting lighter and then darker outside, but we didn't have any way of keeping track. Time just seemed to pass.

Don't think I decided we were stuck and never worried about it. I worried. Believe me, I worried. At some point, though, there didn't seem to be any point to worrying anymore and I kind of settled down. I really did try to get out, at first, but stopped when it was clear I wasn't getting out. I assumed the same happened to Thomas and Kate.

In fact, our food hadn't even come yet when I tried to get out. The first time we ordered, mind you, back before I realized anything weird was going on, Kate let slip why they'd invited me out to lunch: Daedalus, my dog. I headed right for the exit; didn't even say a word in response.

Of course, it wasn't that easy. It couldn't have been, could it? Otherwise I would have walked out and there wouldn't have been any more to the story.

No, when I tried to storm out of the Village Inn at that point, I smacked right into the door. I put out my hand and was stomping so fast that when the door didn't open my elbow bent and I ran into the glass.

For a second, I was embarrassed. However, there was no one in the entryway. Not at the hostess stand, the register, or even the pie case. Embarrassing, but it's not like anyone saw me. I had to remind myself that I was supposed to be pissed.

Anyway, I assumed that door was locked and tried the other one. Those doors were supposed to stay unlocked during business hours, right? Well, I figured maybe that one was broken and they locked it, forgetting to put up a sign. Or, maybe some asshole had pulled the sign down. I figured I should let them know, but I really just wanted out of there. Maybe even more so than before.

But when I tried the other door, it didn't move either. I don't mean like it moved and then the lock caught; I mean it didn't budge at all.

Okay, I know what you're thinking. You're thinking of that Far Side cartoon where the kid is pushing on a door marked 'PULL' on the side of a building with a School for the Gifted sign on it. I'm right, aren't I?

Well, you're wrong. I pushed on both doors. I pulled. I even pushed and then pulled, and pulled and then pushed. They're doors, right? I kept thinking I was doing something wrong.

I even looked around the place to make sure it wasn't getting robbed. Maybe they locked all the doors under orders from robbers. But, if it was, I couldn't see it. Everyone was eating and walking around like normal. Certainly, I didn't see any guys in ski masks or stockings or anything like that. Definitely no guns visible.

Frankly, it didn't even look like the doors were locked. I could see right through the gap between the doors where the deadbolt would go. Nothing. I looked for any other kind of lock, but everything I could find was unlocked, too. No, those doors couldn't have been locked.

Except... they wouldn't open.

My next thought, and I thought it was a pretty good one, was to get someone. As I said before, though, nobody was around. It was weird. After all, how many times do you walk into a Village Inn and not see someone at the pie counter, or the register, or the hostess stand? Not often. Sure, it happens from time to time, but not for that long at a stretch. Sooner or later, somebody should have gravitated up to the front.

But they didn't. I sat and waited for a while on the bench inside the inner set of doors, but no one ever came. To be honest, it freaked me out a little.

Eventually, I decided I had to go and get someone. After all, sooner or later Kate and Thomas would decide to leave as well. I didn't really want to run into them again in the entryway, not after having stormed off. It would have ruined a good angry exit. Besides, they'd probably think I had something to do with the doors.

So, I took the initiative and went to grab a waitress. Easy, right? There were waitresses running all around the dining area. All I had to do was catch one and demand that she open the doors. If anyone went toward the front then she'd just be first priority. Not a big deal at all.

Of course, I picked a waitress who wasn't near the booth where Kate and Thomas were still sitting. I didn't even want to know what it would look like, after having me run out, to see me chasing waitresses around. I had pride, after all.

Luckily, there was a waitress pouring coffee at a table all the way on the other side of the dining room from Kate and Thomas. Deciding she'd do, I made a beeline for her. However, right as I was getting close, she turned and shot right over to Kate and Thomas's booth. Still trying to avoid them, I backed off.

That was strange on its own. She wasn't our waitress and she was stopping by to top off coffee. Worse, as I'm pretty sure I mentioned before, I was the only one drinking coffee. Unless they expected me to come slinking back, which wasn't likely, there was no need for more coffee, especially since my cup had been full when I'd left. Nothing to fill.

That's when I saw a gaggle of old blue-hairs leaving in a big bunch. I took off running for the front because they walked right out without any trouble at all. Figuring someone must have fixed the doors when I wasn't looking, I ran.

Incidentally, I probably should have still checked the doors that time before trying to fly right through again. I didn't think I needed to, though. I mean, I saw those old ladies walk right through just a second before. Still, when I got there . . . smack! Again.

Fine. I'd try to catch a waitress again. I didn't even care whether Kate and Thomas saw me, or if I grabbed a waitress right at their booth. By then, I was ready to try just about anything.

It was uncanny, though. The waitresses dashed every which

way, like squirrels on meth. I couldn't catch one no matter how fast I ran. I'd see one, but then she'd be gone. I chased one around a table, her not looking at me once, before she finally took off into the back.

Frustration overcame my anger and, frankly, I was getting pretty winded. My Nike sweat suit wasn't exactly purchased for working out.

I did a little experiment and approached a waitress not intending to say anything about the door. Thinking she was going to run off, I ran right into her. "Watch it!" I yelled.

Thinking quick, I decided to switch and ask about the door anyway. That's when this sound of tons of glasses hitting concrete erupted out of the back. Of course, she ran off. "Hey!" I called after her, but she was gone. Didn't look back once.

I'll spare you most of what happened after that, since it was all pretty much the same as what went before. I couldn't catch a waitress if I wanted to ask. I could if I didn't, but they always seemed to have a really good reason to be gone, unstoppably so, if I switched. People came and went, too, though the doors were immovable again by the time I could get to them. Nobody came or went if I waited close enough to the doors.

Finally, I gave up. After all, it was pretty obvious that I wasn't getting out, whatever the reason. Eventually, when I wasn't pissed anymore and really didn't care what Kate and Thomas would say, I sat back down at the booth.

It was as if I'd never been gone, though food had arrived. Kate and Thomas just ate. They didn't mention anything about me leaving or coming back.

Beverages

I like to make up stories for people. Wild, exciting things that couldn't possibly have happened. Anything realistic isn't any fun, and the more interesting the better. Also, the less actually connected to the factual people, the better.

My histories are much more interesting than what actually happened. Who cares that the bus driver on the number two route has driven the same bus for 30 or more ungodly years because he's a hard worker? Boring! I'm much more interested in the possible fact that he once sold the red Chinese the secret of manufacturing mercury amalgam dental fillings to pay for his daughter to go to Juilliard.

Anyway, the things I make up feel truer about the various people involved, whoever they happen to be, than the actual things that happened to them. The fact that the night clerk at 7-11 collects baseball cards conveys nothing of his real essence. Now, the fact that he also collects copper nails from electrical poles in order to fashion graven images as commanded by a secret cult of fisherman working to bring about the return of Baal brings forth that essence, even if there is no way that he really does that. Not that I'd bother to find out if he did. That'd just ruin things.

See what I mean?

Now, I'm telling you this because I sat in that booth for a very, very long time. I got bored. I got very, very bored. I made up a lot of stories. I'm going to share a few of them.

For the time being, I'll tell you about Alphonse. He was the dishwasher, back in the kitchen.

Let me back up.

You see, I never went into the kitchen there. We did everything else, but none of us went back in the kitchen. Maybe I didn't feel so bold after all the trouble with the front doors. The kitchen just didn't interest me much.

Obviously, since I never went in back, I really didn't know who all was back there. There could have been an entire high school marching band doing nude aerobics in the kitchen; I wouldn't have known a thing about it. Cooks, dishwashers, or whatever, I had no way of knowing whether or not they were back there.

At the same time, they had to be. Right? Food came out. Therefore, somebody had to have cooked it. The food was circumstantial proof of the existence of cooks as there could have been no food otherwise.

So, having proved the existence of the cooks, we can similarly deduce the existence of at least one dishwasher. After all, the food was served on dishes. Clean dishes. Either they had an infinite supply stashed somewhere back there or somebody, the dishwasher, was transforming the dirty ones into clean.

Assuming the existence of the dishwasher as a priori, we will call him Alphonse. We shall do so because, not having proof of his certain materiality, that is what I named him. I like the sound of it. It gives him a certain flair no other dishwasher could possibly possess. If he was actually named something else then that just shows that his parents got it wrong. Obviously.

Okay, so, a dishwasher named Alphonse. Alphonse, washer of dishes. Dishes washed by Alphonse.

Of course, Alphonse was not born a dishwasher. Very few people are. I suspect it has something to do with OSHA regulations. Alphonse was actually born a prince. The dishwasher thing came later, something that developed over time.

Alphonse was a prince of some tiny European country you've never had cause to think about, like Lichtenstein. Or France. Some place where they don't even have princes anymore, but did when Alphonse was born.

When Alphonse was a child, his favorite thing to do was sit in one of the many rooms of the royal castle where the family dish sets were displayed. Old dishes. Sets of dishes passed down through Alphonse's family since the Middle Ages. Beautiful dishes, painted like illuminated manuscripts depicting scenes like young lovers courting and bosom friends celebrating at feasts.

Alphonse used to be able to waste whole days like that, sitting among the displayed dishes until one of his many nannies came and forcibly removed him for dinner or a dress ball, or some other such royal thing. Left on his own, he would have stayed there forever. He would have just stared, dreaming.

You see, the dishes were people to Alphonse. Tiny porcelain people. In sets they were families, clans. They lived little dish lives and achieved little dish achievements. He even gave them little dish names; perhaps names like Kate and Thomas. But, unlike the dishes at the dinner table, they were perfect and unspoiled. Unlike the world outside those rooms, they were finished and never changed. Alphonse couldn't possibly imagine anything better.

Of course, things didn't stay that way. They couldn't have or Alphonse would never have become the dishwasher. One day, there was a revolt.

The details of the revolt aren't important as far as I'm concerned, people ruining a perfectly pleasant situation like good relationships, and it would bore me to dream up any details about that. Alphonse was too young to understand them anyway. Besides, most revolts are pretty similar. If you've studied one revolt then you've studied them all. Suffice it to say, Alphonse and his family were thrown out of the country and had to flee to America. He wasn't a prince anymore. Or, well, I guess he was still a prince. He just wasn't a prince of anything in particular.

Regardless, Alphonse didn't care about all that. He cared about what happened to the dishes.

That was the worst part. When his family fled, they had to leave all the dishes behind. The revolters stole them along with everything else the royal family had. They might have been smashed to pieces or broken up into lots and sold, scattered the world over. Alphonse didn't know; he just knew the dishes were gone.

Of course, Alphonse was heartbroken. Who wouldn't be? He thought those dishes would always be there. They were part of his birthright, a tangible symbol to him of the kingdom he was to have. He couldn't imagine the world without them.

For years, or what seemed like years, Alphonse did nothing. He just sat around remembering, but remembering wasn't good enough. Remembering only reminded him of what he had lost, reminded him of the horrible truth about the world.

Frankly, he didn't see much point in going on. Would you? When everything you have ever loved is gone? I wouldn't. Mind you, I primarily ate off paper plates at home and didn't even have a full dish set, much less a nice one, but I still think I know what Alphonse felt.

Alphonse was empty, but he didn't kill himself. Maybe he had some kind of inner prince-like fortitude.

As I said before, Alphonse did nothing. But . . . one day his mailman saw him. Now, you might find this a bit hard to believe, but his mailman was a prince, too. It's true; there are far more secret princes out there than you might think, and they all know each other. With all the revolutions that have happened, they've gotten scattered all over the place. You'd never notice them, but they keep track of each other and hang out sometimes—be princes together.

The mailman took pity on Alphonse, what with the state Alphonse was in. I mean, he was a prince, too. He'd probably lost things he loved in revolts as well. Of all people, he could understand what Alphonse was going through.

Still, pity or no, the mailman-prince knew he couldn't fix things for Alphonse. Things had gone too far for that and the mailman-prince didn't have any power. He knew Alphonse could not undo the past, and he knew Alphonse would probably never be rich enough again to assemble those kind of dishes together. But, he did have at least one good idea.

He told Alphonse to get a job as a dishwasher. That would not give Alphonse his own dishes to keep, but it would give him a chance to be near as many dishes as possible. He would even get to care for them, to love them. It might not have been perfect, but it was the best thing under the circumstances.

Alphonse jumped at the idea. He hadn't thought such a thing was even still possible. What can I say? I think there was something a little wrong with Alphonse, too many generations of royal inbreeding maybe.

He could see it all in his head right then, dishes upon dishes upon dishes. They'd be arranged in orderly stacks, dinner plates with dinner plates and soup bowls with soup bowls. He didn't care about silverware so much, his love only extended to dishes, but he'd care for that as well. They'd be perfect and they'd be clean, all because of Alphonse.

He ran out and got a job at the Village Inn that day, the same Village Inn I later got trapped at. There was no connection; he'd been there for 20 years or more before I ever walked into those damned doors.

Actually, though, it wasn't as perfect as Alphonse thought it would be. He'd clean and clean and clean, dreaming of having all the dishes washed and arranged into little families and clans. However, the cooks had different ideas.

After all, the task of a cook is to prepare and serve food. That is what they must do. So, as soon as Alphonse finished washing a dish, the cooks would take it from him. They took it and they served food on it. As a result, the dish was suddenly as dirty as it had been before.

The cycle went on endlessly. Alphonse washed. The cooks cooked. Then Alphonse washed more. Then the cooks cooked some more. Each kept pace with the other and nobody got ahead. Sometimes the dishes were even broken in the line of duty and new ones had to be ordered. It was certainly nothing like the idyllic days of Alphonse's youth, repetitive futility as opposed to the peaceful moments of stillness when he used to sit and stare at the beautiful scenes painted on his perfect dishes.

Yet, Alphonse was happy in his new life. He did not blame the cooks for fighting so hard against him. That was just their way, and he forgave them for it.

And it wasn't always like that. Sometimes, when he cleaned very, very hard, he occasionally got ahead of the cooks. It may have only been for a short while, but it was heaven while it lasted. And sometimes, just sometimes, Alphonse would come in when the Village Inn was closed, though it never seemed to while I was there, so he could sit alone with his dishes.

Things were quiet when he sat with his dishes alone in the closed Village Inn. The dishes were all clean then, since there was no one to order food and no cooks to cook it. He'd take all the dishes down from their racks and shelves and stack them all up together on the floor around him. For a little while, until he had to put the dishes back away and go home, it was as if he was a child again, at home in the royal castle.

MONDAY

Breakfast

"What would you bring," I asked, "if you were stuck in a Village Inn?"

Thomas had been singing "One Hundred Bottles of Beer on the Wall" yet again. I had to do something to put a stop to that. Kate was brushing her teeth with her finger. The impromptu dental hygiene was bad enough, but I had to do something about the singing.

Contrary to common understanding, monotonous songs do not pass time. In fact, they stretch it out to incomprehensible lengths. I'm not sure why this is so, but it is. Perhaps it is some as of yet undiscovered phenomenon of physics. Regardless, the singing made an already bad situation downright unbearable. The fact that it was Thomas singing didn't help matters any.

"Is this like that what would you bring to a deserted island game?" Thomas asked, thankfully abandoning the song. "I hate that game. They always used to make us play it at day camp when I was a kid. Totally freaked me out, because we always went on a hike after that."

"At least it would have just been the woods." Kate smiled at him. "You could have walked home."

"That's not the point. Anyway," he said, looking at me, "is that the game here?"

"Similar, but different. No desert island is involved, just what you would bring if you knew you were going to be stuck in a Village Inn. It's the same basic concept, but with a totally different scenario."

"We are in a Village Inn," Kate grumped.

I shot her a nasty look. "Exactly. That's what makes this version so unique. We have an unusual perspective."

"So people should play the game when actually stranded on a deserted island?" Kate smirked. "See what they should have thought to take with them? Seems a bit far to go for a parlor game."

I smiled. "Double exactly. We don't have to go through any extra effort; we're already here. There seems to be a dearth of deserted islands within easy reach anyway. Village Inns, however, are pretty conveniently located."

"Especially for us," she replied.

"Especially for us. The real difference, though, is most people that play the island version have no experience at all of being on a desert island. They have to completely imagine the whole situation, which can't be what it would really be like in the slightest. As a result, the things they would bring couldn't be even remotely useful."

"I thought that was the point."

"For the island version," I agreed, "not this one. We have actual insight into the situation and to what we really wish we had brought—the benefit of hindsight. Now we can see how the results differ from the standard way the game is played."

"Do we each name something and then the next person has to remember that along with all the things mentioned before, adding a new item to the list?" Thomas asked, cringing. "I'm not good with lists. Always hated that part the most."

"We can nix that part of the game," Kate suggested. "We might as well, since we're changing the basic underlying premise anyway. What's one more thing?"

I shrugged. "Sure. The interesting part is the effect of hindsight. I really don't care how many objects we can all remember."

We all sat there for a bit. It wasn't like we were in a hurry, but everyone seemed to be waiting for someone else to kick it all off. I didn't think I should go first because the game was my idea. It'd seem like a justification to talk and then they probably wouldn't really get involved, just tune out. No moving things forward that way.

Kate elbowed Thomas. "Go."

"Why me?" he whined, rubbing the now sore spot on his ribs.

"Consider it prevention against just ditching you in the

woods," she replied, smirking at Thomas. "That still isn't totally impossible, though it would take some doing. Just go and don't tempt us to think of a way."

"All right, all right," Thomas protested. He looked around the restaurant. His eyes settled on the pie menu sitting on the back edge of the table. Reaching over to snag it, he started flipping aimlessly. I doubted he was considering ordering any more at that moment. Maybe he was considering the existence of the pies.

"Well," he said finally, snapping shut the menu, "I'll tell you one thing I wouldn't bring. Food. It doesn't seem like that would be necessary."

"One big difference from the desert island scenario," I agreed, "but how about something you actually would bring?"

"Okay," he said, rolling his neck and massaging it with one hand, "pillows."

"Pillows?"

"Yeah," he continued. "Maybe some blankets. These booths aren't bad, but there are limits to how long they're comfortable. If I had a pillow, I could wedge it by the wall and spread out better. That's essential."

"I'd just lay my head on your lap and stretch out whether I had a pillow or not." Kate smiled sweetly at him, tilting her head. "I'm better positioned, being on the outside."

Thomas put a hand around her narrow waist and squeezed. "Not just one pillow either, I'd need a variety. A good pillow selection would be ideal so I could fit the pillow to my mood. A body pillow, a reading pillow, a normal sleeping pillow, maybe even a couple of throw pillows just to cover all the bases."

"Village Inn should think about adding a pillow menu," Kate suggested. "Seems like that might be a hit. They could keep it in the holder with the pie menu."

My fingers drummed manically on the tabletop. I noticed and stopped myself. "That's interesting. Out of all the things I expected, I never guessed pillows would be the first thing you'd pick."

"I could use one right now." Thomas grinned sheepishly.

"And what's wrong with pillows?" Kate asked. She cocked her

head like she was innocently curious, but I knew she only did that when she was baiting somebody.

"It isn't exactly survival-oriented," I calmly explained. "Pillows may be useful for long term comfort, but they'd hardly mean the difference between life and death."

"Maybe switching the game from a desert island to a Village Inn just does that," she countered. "Maybe you've removed the idea of mortal danger that's inherent in the game."

I had to admit she had a point, though I wasn't happy about Kate having a point. Still, that was the kind of insight I'd been looking for.

"How about you?" Thomas challenged me. "What would you bring?"

Kate leaned back into the cushion of the booth seat, sitting up very straight. I knew she was getting ready for something. I decided to be very careful about my answer. Her and Thomas looked at me.

"Vodka," I replied. "One thing this place lacks is liquor. I'm betting it would be a whole lot more enjoyable if I were hammered. I'd certainly be able to survive it better that way."

Thomas nodded, snorting lightly with unreleased laughter. There might have been some humor there, but there was truth as well. I could have gone for some vodka.

"Okay," Kate said quickly, a bit of a sharp tone in her voice, "you'd bring pillows and you'd bring booze. Is it my turn now?" She addressed us both, but only looked at me.

"Go ahead," I said, leaning back as well. Time to see what she was up to.

"I'd bring Daedalus." She smiled, looking very pleased with herself.

Daedalus, my dachshund. Or, perhaps more accurately, mine and Thomas's dachshund. The exact status of Daedalus was a matter of no little debate between the three of us.

"You're a bitch," I told her.

Lunch

Enough about Daedalus for the moment. I didn't want to talk about Daedalus.

I was sprawled across the bench on my side of the booth. My head dangled down off the end. One foot was draped over the back of my seat and the other rested on the wall. I had one arm up over my chest. The other hung down under the table. My body stayed motionless.

Kate and Thomas didn't move either. They were both half sat up, but Kate was flopped back over the seat of their side of the booth, arms flung wide, and Thomas leaned against the wall in a crumpled sort of fashion. His back was twisted, probably missing those pillows he talked about earlier. Their bodies breathed, but that was about it. I was impressed with their level of commitment.

The Village Inn operated all around us. People ate. They finished and left. Other people sat down and ordered. Waitresses wandered around. Some of them brought food to tables. People went to the bathroom. People came back from the bathroom. A shrunken blue-haired old lady nearby debated loudly whether to get the buttermilk pancakes or whether to be 'healthy' and get the multigrain option, as if that helped when smothered in butter and syrup. In short, life inside the Village Inn continued.

"Are you people okay?" Sherri, our waitress, didn't sound all that concerned. I was sure she thought we were just screwing around. We were, after all.

At least, she was Sherri according to her little plastic nametag. That was the only reason I knew her name. I found myself wondering if there was anything to stop her from using someone else's nametag. Then she could pretend to be a totally different waitress, whatever advantage there might have been in being a different waitress.

"We're fine," I explained, moving as little as I had to in order to speak. I figured if we didn't acknowledge her then she'd actually have to do something. Escalate the situation. She probably had enough to worry about without getting involved with us.

Sherri seemed like a high school version of Kate or me, had Kate or me ever been a short and pudgy Latino girl with drawn-on Star Trek villainess eyebrows and silver-colored dream catcher earrings. Come to think of it, she was nothing like either Kate or me.

She probably spent her off hours watching Geraldo and driving around some boyfriend who lost his license due to too many DUIs. Or, at the very least, collected Beanie Babies. Still, she treated us pretty good. I probably wouldn't have.

"Can I get you anything else right now?

"We could use some refills," I suggested.

Need would have been the wrong word to use. We weren't dry by any means, though our glasses weren't completely full. Refills would certainly be convenient at some point in the future beyond that particular time, but there was no immediacy necessary.

Besides, what did dead people, or living people pretending to be dead like we were, need with refills? They couldn't drink, and would have no need of either thirst quenching or hydration. So, technically, we couldn't really 'use' the new refills. We may have wanted them, but would have had to be done pretending to be dead before we could make any real use out of them.

Sherri was a good egg. Whether we were pretending to be dead or not, she still brought us the refills. Maybe it was even more convenient for her. After all, draped all over the place as we were, we weren't in the way when she reached around the table. It's because we were always such good customers.

Whatever we were wrapped up in at that Village Inn, Sherri seemed to be part of it. She'd been there since just after we'd sat down. In getting our drink order, she must have gotten pulled into whatever it was with us. Not all the time, but often. Sometimes she was at other tables, or maybe back in the kitchen or break room since we didn't see her, but she never switched off with anybody else. She never got to go home. And, the worst part, since we never got a bill, she never got tipped.

I felt worse for her than I did for us, or at least worse than I did for Kate and Thomas. After all, she had to work. We may have been stuck, too, but we just had to hang out and sometimes eat something. Waiting tables for endless years must have been hell, though she didn't have to spend all that time with her ex and his new girlfriend, who also happened to be her ex-best friend.

"You're not as dead as we are," Kate insisted. "You talked to Sherri. You can't be completely dead if you were doing that. There must still be life in you."

Playing dead was Daedalus's favorite trick. Well, it was his only trick, really. Supposedly he could shake, fetch, and do a few other things, but he'd only remember how to do those once in a while. Playing dead he had down, though. Half the time you'd tell him to do something else and he'd play dead instead. I'm not sure if he got confused or if he thought that would satisfy, or if he were just hoping we'd think he really was dead and therefore excuse him from the expected trick. His paws always twitched when he played dead.

We were playing dead because we all missed Daedalus. It hadn't been exactly phrased like that, but that was the general idea behind our apparent lifelessness. That and the fact that it felt good to be in a different position for a while.

"I was communicating from the great beyond," I countered. "That means I'm just as dead as you guys, if not more so since you were both alive enough to make the conscious decision not to respond to her. I merely had a message for the living and my spirit couldn't rest until it was delivered."

"Concerning refills?"

"I will not have the motives of my spirit called into question. The ways of those who have passed on are a mystery to the living." I closed my eyes. It seemed more real if I closed them.

"Aren't you supposed to communicate through tapping or Ouija boards or something?" Kate chimed in.

"Some spirits can talk to the living," I replied. "Besides, tapping and such like that are parlor tricks. This is a Village Inn, not a parlor."

"I stand corrected," Kate conceded.

"Dead people don't stand," I replied. "I must be deader than you because I wouldn't stand for anything."

"Figure of speech. Anyway, I'm the deadest because I've got rigor mortis," she said, stiffening.

"No," Thomas countered, "I'm the deadest. I've even started to smell."

"You smelled when you were alive."

"It's true," I agreed.

"I'm dead to the world," Kate moaned.

"I'm dead to rights," I offered.

"I'm dead glad to meet you both," Thomas drawled in his best Texas accent, which sounded more like a Canadian version of Pee-wee Herman.

Having beaten the life out of that joke, the conversation went dead silent. We seemed to be getting bored of being dead, which wasn't a good thing. We were already bored enough of being alive, and there were only so many options.

"Our deaths need backgrounds to be believable," I suggested. "Motivation. What did you each die of? You'll be deader if you pin it down."

Kate sighed. "You first this time. It's got to be your turn by now."

"Fine. I'm a recently widowed church-going old lady. When my husband died, I turned myself into a shut-in."

"What?" Kate asked, incredulous. "That's it? I bet you died of a heart attack and nobody found you for weeks. That's just lame."

"Let me finish. The other church-going ladies all felt sorry for me and a group of them dragged me out to a Village Inn. They ordered for me and made me eat everything on their plate because they kept confusing me with their grandchildren. Worse, they all had dementia and kept forgetting they'd made me eat already so they ordered more."

"Better," Kate agreed. "Continue."

"Glad to. Finally, after having consumed enough pancakes

and sausage to power New York City for a week via biofuel, they let me go back to my tiny, one-bedroom apartment... which happened to be a fifth-floor walkup."

"Ooh," Thomas interrupted, "and you died of an aneurism trying to struggle up the stairs like that."

"Not so fast," I snapped. "I got home, but another group of the church-going ladies was waiting. Not knowing about the other group taking me out already, they forced me to go to a Six Flags to cheer me up. They didn't even ride any rides; they just put me on and watched."

"Did you protest?" Kate asked.

"Couldn't. I was too full to talk. Anyway, none of them would have heard me. They were all deaf."

"So," Kate griped, "when's the death part come in? You'll die of natural causes at this rate."

"I'm getting there, but I'll speed it up in case you've got something pressing to get to. Stuffed full like that and throttled by roller coaster after roller coaster, the pressure burst my intestines. I died of internal bleeding on the merry-go-round."

"Wow. Nice touch," Kate conceded.

"Thanks," I replied. "Anyway, the old ladies didn't even notice. I wasn't talking before and hadn't been moving too good because of all that food, so the old ladies thought I'd just had too much fun and took me home. Plopped me right on the couch."

"And then you rotted for several weeks before anyone discovered you because the old church ladies forgot about you, since they had dementia and all, right?"

"Yup."

"I knew that part was coming," Kate complained.

"Hey," I countered, "I can decompose if I want to. The customer is always right."

"I'm a customer, too," Kate pointed out. "What happens if we disagree?"

"Then that means it's my turn," Thomas said.

I felt somebody walk by the booth. Thinking it was our waitress, I opened my eyes. It wasn't, though, just some fat guy in a too-small t-shirt on his way to the bathroom, so I closed them again. I was dead after all.

"Okay," I told him, "go ahead and die."

"Very kind of you. Okay, I was your neighbor across the hall. It was an old building, poorly put together. There was this huge gap under the door. All that time you were rotting over in your apartment, the bacteria and germs poured off of your corpse onto the floor and got blown by a bad draft under your door, into my apartment."

"I told you door runners weren't just decorations," Kate remarked. "You should have gotten one."

"I'm a guy," he explained, "I never got around to it. Wouldn't even know where they sold them."

Kate tsked.

"I know. At first I got the sniffles and thought it was just the flu. The body aches got worse as the contagion kept spreading and I knocked myself out on entire bottles of NyQuil. I was so out of it that I didn't realize it was actually cholera. Of course, I died before I managed to sober up and figure out what was going on."

"Cut down in your prime," Kate crooned. "Such bad luck, especially since cholera isn't usually airborne."

"All because Cassandra had to go and be dead 20 feet away from my door."

"My bad," I said.

"Couldn't be helped," he remarked magnanimously. "How about you, Kate? What'd you die of? Industrial accident? Freak piano explosion?"

"Neglect," she replied coldly.

"Ouch," I said.

"I was Thomas's ward. He took good care of me, dressed me in little blue pinafore dresses, but then he caught the plague from your corpse and died."

"Happens to the best of us," Thomas offered.

"Yes, well, social services came and claimed me, but all the foster homes were full. I slept on a desk in their office for a week. Finally, they sent me to live with a cloister of nuns who'd all lost their faith and only took me in because they needed the money."

"Wait," Thomas interrupted. "You were my ward? Why didn't you do something when I was dying of cholera? That would have been a good time to speak up. Maybe call 911 or something. Get a neighbor at least."

"I was too young to know how to dial for help. I was helpless as a little puppy. Anyway, the neighbor was a decomposing corpse and you were hammered, remember?"

"Right. Sorry about that."

"Nothing you could do. To get back to the story, though, the nuns kept me in a closet and only fed me every third Tuesday, plus extra food on holy days. Eventually, they got engrossed in a Matlock marathon and forgot me entirely."

"The fate of so many," I remarked.

"My weak little system just couldn't take it. I died weeks later from a combination of starvation, scurvy, and an untreated hangnail."

"Not bad," I conceded.

"It all could have been prevented," she went on. "If only Thomas had been able to care for me. If only you hadn't had to kill him by dying."

"Yup, it sucks," I agreed quickly, not playing into her game. "Hey, does anybody feel like some toast? I bet they'll serve us a side by itself if we ask."

Dinner

"Hey, what do you guys think of—"

"You're always thinking of things," Kate snapped. "Other people have ideas, too. For once, I have something kooky and you're both going to do it."

"Okay," I said, holding up my hands with my palms facing her, the universal 'take it easy' sign. "Your turn, go ahead."

"I'm game," Thomas agreed, nodding.

Kate nodded as well, though I wasn't sure if she was agreeing with herself or with Thomas's agreement, or just nodding because she was surprised we gave in so easily. Either way, it looked a little odd.

"We're going to have a debate," she finally continued. "You're going to state a position why one of the breakfast meats is superior to the others. Then, you're going to defend your choice."

Frankly, this one felt like something we'd already done before. I'm pretty sure it was even my idea at the time. I wasn't going to say anything, though. She sat rigid, arms crossed across her chest and chin pointed up haughtily. Hostile. There was no way I was going to deliberately set her off.

"Does corned beef hash count?" Thomas asked.

"No," Kate snapped, "That's a breakfast meal that contains a meat. It's got potato chunks in it even before the addition of any sides. You can pick just the corned beef part if you want, but corned beef by itself isn't very breakfast-y. I don't think it would do very well."

Thomas reached for the menu we still had sitting on the table. He studied it, probably preparing his argument or trying to make it seem like the argument he was going to present was based on solid, indisputable facts obtained from the Village Inn menu. As if the VI menu had those kinds of facts. It was a little silly either way; this wasn't that kind of debate.

"And breakfast meats can't borrow any grace from the things they're often served with," Kate barked. "The different things that can be paired with a meat may be persuasive evidence of its higher qualities, but by themselves they can't establish that the meat is better or worse than another."

"Got it," Thomas replied.

"I'll pick ham steak," I offered, hoping to get things started and to get her to chill out a little. Thomas closed the menu and set it back on the table. "I don't think you can really attack ham steak, not and still be able to sleep at night."

"And what's so great about ham steak?" Kate demanded.

"Think about it," I replied. "Ham steak is the core of the Ultimate Breakfast. The name obviously says it all, and the bacon and sausage are just condiments. Accessories, if you will. The ham is the one that is the key player, the lynch pin of the whole operation."

"What about steak in steak and eggs?" Kate challenged, smiling with what she must have thought was an obvious easy victory. As if I hadn't prepared for that.

"The steak in steak and eggs is usually the worst cut you can get, often a tough flank steak or some such thing. VI does a bit better, but it's still a breakfast steak. Even if it wasn't, it still carries the stigma from restaurants where it is. Ham steak, on the other hand, is the best possible cut of ham you can get. The zenith. It's tasty, not composed of ground-up assorted things, and not over half-made of fat globs. Clearly, it's the Cadillac of the breakfast meat kingdom."

"What about chicken fried steak?" Thomas asked, joining the debate a little late in my opinion. "It's the center of its own meal, and it doesn't get any better than the breakfast version."

"Don't make me laugh," I countered, deliberately using the tired old joke. "Chicken fried steak . . . if it was so great, why does it have to hide under all that breading? Is it afraid to show itself? What has it got to hide? There must be something under there that no one wants us to know about. Something horrible, like Nazi tattoos."

"Hey," Thomas interrupted, "don't get so defensive. That isn't my pick. I was just playing chicken fried steak advocate a bit."

"Ham steak has no reason to hide," I continued. "It's perfectly fine with its body image and isn't ashamed of anything. There isn't even any need for gravy, particularly one with another meat in it, as if it wasn't enough on its own."

"But," Kate reminded, "it is often served with bacon and sausage. Whether you consider them merely accessories or not, the fact of the supplementation is still there. Ham steak is rarely, if ever, served completely alone."

"That isn't due to any defect in the ham steak," I protested. "Bacon and sausage are groupies, hangers-on. They just keep showing up, whether the ham steak wants them there or not. Ham steak is certainly gracious about it, sharing the spotlight that really only it deserves, but they are still Rob Schneider and Norm MacDonald to the ham steak's Adam Sandler."

Thomas laughed. "I can't believe you worked a Rob Schneider reference in there."

"I take my ham steak very seriously."

Kate rolled her eyes. "All right, enough with the ham steak. It's getting old. Let's move on to Thomas."

We both turned and he pretended to pull his collar away from his neck and cough. Mind you, collared shirts were not typical operating procedure for Thomas. He was usually more into the overall urban-slacker look, whatever jeans and t-shirt happened to be within reach. Grey checkered Abercrombie & Fitch gear was particularly uncharacteristic, as were dark khaki chinos. I seriously suspected Kate was sinisterly involved . . . changing him.

"Sure you're not going for chicken fried steak?" I asked him. "You can still pick that one, even though I've thoroughly trashed it already. I'm sure we can pretend like there's still some room for debate."

"No need," Thomas reassured, "it really wasn't mine."

"Of course you'd say that now," I teased.

"No, really. I picked bacon. Who wouldn't?"

Kate raised an eyebrow, clearly deliberately since it was only the one. "Even after Cassandra declared it was a mere condiment?"

"Changes nothing," Thomas concluded. "Bacon is still the holy grail of meats, breakfast or otherwise. Cassandra can have her opinion; I'll keep my bacon."

"I respect your right to your bacon," Kate offered.

"I wouldn't dream of denying Thomas bacon," I told Kate, "but he needs more than blind religious fervor. It isn't persuasive if we aren't bacon-devotees already."

"Well," Thomas replied, "you can't deny the flavor of the bacon. It's at least a close relative of the ham steak so you'd have to go back on your own argument if you did that."

"Wouldn't think of it. Though, nothing prevents me from preferring the ham steak. Mere family relation is the difference between Sylvester Stallone and his brother Frank."

"Duly noted," he continued, "but you at least accept the compelling flavor. In fact, the flavor is so compelling that it can improve virtually any food. Bacon on burgers, bacon in potato soup, even bacon in chocolate."

"Bacon does not improve chocolate," Kate insisted. "I'm calling that one. Try something else."

"Bacon improves filet mignon," he offered.

Kate and I both nodded, offering no challenge to the replacement suggestion. Various meats could be wrapped in bacon for flavor boost. That fact was simply not disputable.

"Not only is bacon added to other dishes, it significantly improves those foods. It isn't merely served with them by custom. Instead, bacon is widely regarded as an enhancement."

"Ham is also used for flavoring," I quipped.

"Sure," he admitted, "in a few things. Split pea soup. Bean soup. However, it has neither the same scope of use as bacon nor the same reputation. Plus, bacon adds a more distinctive flavor for the same amount."

Damn. Thomas actually had a pretty good argument. I started wishing I'd picked bacon. Why'd I pick ham? I couldn't even remember anymore.

"What about the fat?" I asked. "Bacon is usually mostly fat with just a little bit of meat." I was trying, but my heart wasn't really on board. My heart was down with the bacon.

"Doesn't matter," he countered. "It's still fried crispy so it's delicious, not like the limp, gooey fat on ham. That stuff has the texture of congealed mucus."

That did it. Any comparison to mucus won the argument. At that moment, I wouldn't ever eat ham steak again, though I probably would as soon as I'd forgotten about the comparison.

"In fact," Thomas continued, "I could go for a side of bacon right about now." He tried to signal the waitress.

"Okay," Kate concluded. "I think we're going to have to agree that bacon beats ham steak since Thomas is willing to eat some right now to prove his point. If I ate right now I'd puke."

"I'll retract my position as long as I don't have to have any of it right now. I'm still nauseated from overstuffing myself on our last order."

"We still haven't done mine," Kate reminded. "Don't you guys want to know what I'd pick?"

I looked at her. She'd said it with a deliberately sweet face, which alone signaled trouble. Kate was a lot of things, but sweet wasn't one of them. If it sounded that way then she was faking, usually for a sinister reason. She wasn't exactly a good liar, unlike me.

I was sure I knew what she was doing. She just wouldn't let it die. I didn't want to feed her a line, but we were going to keep dancing around it if I didn't.

"What'd you pick?" I reluctantly asked.

"Sausages," she replied.

"Sausages?"

"Yep. Want to know why?"

I most certainly did not want to know why. I knew already, and I didn't want to know. Still, I was going to have to ask.

"Why?"

"Because." Just the tiniest corners of her 'smile' twisted mockingly. It was a horrible, apocalypse-bringing kind of a fake smile.

"They remind me of dachshunds."

And there we had it, back to that again. "I don't want to talk about dachshunds right now," I grumbled.

"I didn't expect that you did," she replied, sitting back.

Sides

As is probably obvious, this was all originally about Daedalus. That should be clear since I've been talking about him for around three sub-chapters by now. Daedalus, my dachshund. Or, mine and Thomas's dachshund. A shy, smooth-haired tan, miniature dachshund.

Quite a lot of fuss for such a little guy, really. He wouldn't have liked it at all. Conflict tended to make him shiver. He'd try to hide under a blanket if there was too much shouting on the TV, much less in an actual room with him and performed by his owners.

And the ownership was apparently open to debate. It hadn't occurred to me in pre-VI time, but VI time demonstrated the contrary.

By the way, in case it isn't completely apparent, I'd started dividing time up according to whether it was in the Village Inn or prior to the Village Inn, since VI time didn't seem to have any relation to actual time.

It was true; Thomas had been the one to buy Daedalus originally. I won't deny that. And he did play with him from time to time while Thomas and I were still together, though mostly that involved Daedalus playing dead whether instructed to or not.

And it wasn't like Daedalus required a whole lot in the way of care besides companionship, being such a tiny little dog. All you needed to do was toss a little food and water out there once in a while and Daedalus was good. Who can even remember which of us did that on a daily basis? Both? It got done, and it was probably both of us equally if you added it all up. Daedalus certainly didn't starve or die of dehydration after Thomas left.

Though, even Thomas would have to admit that I was always the one to do the walking. Thomas insisted that putting Daedalus out in the yard was enough, since his legs were so short, but Daedalus was fast for being so close to the ground. There was no way that closet-sized yard was all he needed.

I couldn't even keep up with Daedalus on my own. I had to skate around on Rollerblades if I wanted him to be able to run like he could. Unfortunately, Daedalus wasn't strong enough to pull me, even with the skates. He was only a miniature; there was only so much he could do. Still, the skates at least let me keep up without having to kill myself.

So now Kate and Thomas wanted to take Daedalus. Wanted to try to claim that he was only Thomas's dog and so I should hand him over to Thomas. And Kate, as if Kate was even a putative owner of the dog. Or had any kind of link to him.

But that's why we were stuck in the Village Inn. All because they wanted to con me into going out with them so they could butter me up and take my dog. Try to steal him. That's when I walked out, or tried to, when they finally came clean and dropped the dog bombshell. And, that's when we realized we were trapped. Of course, they didn't know that would happen or I doubt even Kate would have set up the lunch.

Regardless, whether Daedalus was my dog or Thomas's and my dog, or whatever, Thomas was the one that left Daedalus when he left. If Daedalus was his and not mine, or both, why didn't he try to take him with? Two people who aren't together obviously can't own the same dog, but Thomas didn't even bring it up. He just took off. It was a bit late to think about it later.

Even my mother had more claim to Daedalus than Kate. He was her 'grandchild'—she even picked out his name. Neither Thomas nor I had thought of one. Supposedly it was because my family was Greek, but Mom was only Greek as far as mythology names and cooking. We didn't break plates at meals or whatever it was real Greeks did.

What kind of Greek names their daughter Cassandra anyway? That always bugged me. I mean, maybe if you'd never read any of the plays it wouldn't be a bad thing, but not if you knew the story at all. It wasn't like Cassandra exactly ended well. I mean, she's murdered.

By the way, don't worry about Daedalus. I just realized you

might think he'd starved to death over at my place, what with me being stuck at the Village Inn for an indeterminate amount of time and all. It was okay; Mom was babysitting. Probably stuffing him full of souvlaki or some other such thing she loved to cook but didn't have anyone to eat it and dachshunds weren't supposed to have.

Maybe we should have let my mom have him if we weren't going to agree. It's not like any of us couldn't live without him, except maybe Mom. As it stood, they were going to keep asking and there was no way I was giving that dog over to Kate.

She already had Thomas. Did she really need another pet? I didn't think so. She could feed Thomas and dress him. Maybe even take him for walks. Get him fixed if she so chose. She didn't need Daedalus on top of all that.

Anyway, who takes someone out to a Village Inn to spring something like that? Nobody. Village Inns are for old people to eat at after church or drunk people to get late-night pancakes; take your pick. They're not for people trying to divide a dog or erase any evidence that a past relationship ever existed. There was probably even something in the Village Inn corporate bylaws to that effect, though Thomas and Kate were obviously unaware of such.

It was kind of funny when I thought about it. We were all there because of Daedalus, but he wasn't even there. Daedalus the dachshund, the elephant in the room who wasn't in the room.

And why did Kate have to keep bringing it up? What did it matter anymore? They couldn't take Daedalus even if they wore me down. We were trapped in a stupid Village Inn! The dog argument wasn't even relevant at that point. Kate kept revisiting it, though. Not all the time, but often enough. A bit too often, to be precise.

I went back and forth on whether I wished Daedalus was there at the Village Inn. I didn't really want him to be trapped as well, and it really wasn't the place for a dog since there was neither dog food nor a place to go potty, but cuddling him would have helped pass the time. Also, a little affection from somebody would have been nice.

I was pretty sure Village Inn wouldn't have let me bring him in anyway, some no dog health code or some such thing. I could have tried arguing he was an assistance animal, but I doubted that they would have bought it. It would have been pretty clear that assistance needed to be provided to Daedalus, not the other way around, and I didn't think that met the definition of an assistance animal. Poor little guy.

If Village Inn had been reasonable, they might have bent the rules since we were stuck in there and couldn't leave. Humanitarian sympathy. However, I didn't know if they even realized we couldn't leave, so that probably wouldn't have worked either.

Why don't they let dogs in restaurants anyway? That's never made sense to me. It's not like people want to take them into the kitchen. That I could see being unsanitary. But the dining room? The food was already on plates. What were the dogs going to do? Maybe they were concerned the dogs might crap on the floor, but they let in babies and I'm sure that happened now and then with them anyway. So why not dogs? It was a mystery.

Anyway, whatever the policy was and the thought process behind it, Daedalus wasn't there. We were, though. We were, and we were arguing about him.

At least, some of the time we were. Other times we did something else. A lot of times we didn't do anything at all. There were an awful lot of times. An awful, awful lot.

Beverages

I was actually planning on telling a made up a story about our waitress here. After all, I let you meet her for the first time in this chapter and it seemed like a good place to tell you a bunch of made up shit about her. However, after a great deal of thorough consideration and a single, momentary whim, I won't.

Sorry, Sherri. I guess you'll have to wait until later. I'll get to back to her, though. I feel like I owe her something, what with her serving us and all and not being able to get any tips. Trust me, she'd been serving us for a long time.

Still, however much I want to do something for our waitress, I feel more like talking about Daedalus. I know I've talked a lot about him, but I still feel like talking more about the cute little guy. Since I hadn't seen him for so long, and since Kate kept bringing him up, I decided to make up something for Daedalus while sitting there in that comfortably cushioned vinyl booth.

Keep in mind, though I tend to make up a lot of different stories about people I run into, or animals for that matter, I don't usually make things up about someone I know quite this well. Certainly not anyone I know well enough to bag their poop. Though that would be a much more intimate level if we were talking about a person instead of a dog, I think the principle is still pretty much the same. If I'm too close then there just isn't any story there.

I don't know what it is; maybe you can't really see the things you're standing next to. Maybe you need distance to be able to be clear. Or, maybe all that real stuff crowds out the stuff you want to imagine, leaving no room at all to dream. Regardless, it's hard.

Luckily for me, no matter how well I knew Daedalus, or anyone for that matter, there were still mysteries. That was the secret, to find some place where the facts didn't shout so loud. A quiet spot inside whomever it was to just sit and think. If I did that, I could make it work. I sometimes had to work to find that place, but there was always something that was still mysterious about everybody.

One of Daedalus's mysteries was where he came from. Thomas brought him home from the downtown animal shelter one day, a rescue. He hadn't been planning it at all. For some reason he could never explain, he walked in the shelter door. When he walked out, he had a dachshund. Life is like that sometimes. That was back when things were going good.

Anyway, we had a dachshund, but we didn't know anything about him. He could have been a former drug mule, or a former business tycoon who got cursed into a dog when his matchstick manufacturing business bulldozed some temperamental fairy's sacred pond to build a new factory. Anything could have happened to him before that day at the shelter; we just didn't know.

And that's what I thought about, sitting there in the booth. I thought about where Daedalus had come from, where he had been before we marched onto the scene. Events had happened, and they weren't normal events at all.

You see, Daedalus hadn't even been born. He was made. In fact, he was a sacred being. A totem. He might have been a being who piddled on the floor if the FedEx guy pounded too hard on the door suddenly, but he was a sacred being who piddled on the floor when the FedEx guy pounded too hard on the door suddenly. It might seem strange, but the strangest things are true.

Daedalus was actually a totem spirit for a race of wind elves that lived on the tops of skyscrapers. They used to live on cliffs and mountaintops, but sometime back they all moved into the cities. Hence, skyscrapers. I'll tell you why later.

The thing that is important right now is that once every hundred years, these elves would gather under a special full moon and make a dog. Of course, they could make a dog out of anything they wanted. That was easy. They did it all the time. They'd just throw some mud together, add some grass for fur, whisper a few elf words, and they'd have a dog. It was only by the light of that special moon, though, that they could embody such a dog with their totem spirit.

It was a really big event in the lives of wind elves. Their whole society was centered on it. In fact, all elven time was counted based on how far they were from the previous special moon. It even zeroed out every time it happened. Their time literally started over. They had no way of keeping track of time that happened before the last one had occurred.

And they each lived about a thousand years, too, so each moon was kind of like Christmas for them. Though, since time started over every hundred years, they had no real way of knowing how old each one of them was or how long roundabout each had left to live. It may seem like an odd way to live to you, but it was the only way the wind elves could think of doing things.

The night they made Daedalus was a big celebration, of course. They gathered the very best mud and grass they could find and kept it moist by sprinkling it, carefully, with the clearest and purest mountain spring water that they could find. Then, singing their low and haunting wind elf songs, they made Daedalus on top of the Empire State Building.

You see, the elves were embroiled in a terrible war with a race of rust gnomes that lived in the sewers of only major cities. The rust gnomes hadn't always lived there, but nobody knew where they'd been before that. They were attracted to humanity, the darkest and most despicable parts hiding inside people, and they moved into the sewers to get closer to man. Some even said they hadn't existed before that; they were actually spawned out of the nastiness of people.

And that's why the wind elves moved from the cliffs and mountains to the tops of high buildings, to get at the rust gnomes. They had to; it was in their blood. They couldn't get too close, because they needed the winds to survive, but if they weren't constantly watching then the gnomes would spread unchecked and we'd all be doomed, doomed by our own darkness.

You see, though the gnomes fed on human darkness, they also drove on and inspired it. The gnomes could secretly influence man, particularly large groups of unquestioning, machine-like men, and they'd use their influence to drive mankind into even more terrible places than it would have gone on its own.

Think about Exxon. Do you really think a corporation would pay that much money to drown Alaska in crude oil? Do you really think they'd hire a drunk captain to be in charge of something that cost so much money? Never, if there were real business principles at work, the actual procedures of a corporation. Corporations make money for shareholders, that's what they were made for. For something like that to happen something has to twist the wheels and cogs out of shape, change the direction of the machinery to do something it was never meant to do, something the corporation would never do on its own because it didn't make the shareholders any money.

That something was the rust gnomes.

Granted, the changes didn't always directly contradict the interests of shareholders. Corporations would catch on and put a stop to the gnomes if they realized what was going on. No, sometimes it was more insidious, twisting the shareholder goals into something that makes money but makes it in a darker way than they otherwise would have. It still hurts the shareholders, but it was so much harder for them to know that something had been at work.

That something was the rust gnomes.

Every horror you've seen on the news that a corporation caused and could not believe, was influenced by something dark to do it. Every CEO that wasted billions of dollars and bankrupted shareholders for no discernible reason, not even to benefit himself, was conned by something. Every board that continued selling a product they knew would kill even though they would be found out and it would destroy the company, did it because of something.

That something was the rust gnomes.

Why else would they do it? The gnomes sat and stewed, dreaming their corruption into human hearts. Then, the darkness from those hearts came back and darkly nourished the gnomes. It would go round and round, decaying into more horribly putrefying sewage, except for the work of the wind elves.

The elves didn't even know why they did it. Really, they would have just as well left man on his own. They had no tie to man, no sacred bond. But, for some reason, perhaps because of the beauty that lived within each elf inherently, they hated the gnomes terribly. Because of that incomprehensible enmity, they liked nothing more than to spoil the pleasure of the gnomes.

And it worked, but the gnomes were very, very powerful. Perhaps they were so powerful because the darker side of our natures was so powerful, but it didn't really matter why. What matters is that the elves needed help. The elves needed an incarnation of their totem spirit in order to be able to mix it up with the gnomes.

Do you remember that's what Daedalus is? See why he's so important for such a little dog?

Of course, since the elves could only make a dog like Daedalus every hundred years, there would be terrible trouble if anything happened to that dog. The Black Death? That was a lost dog. The fall of Rome? Lost dog. The consequences could be unimaginably dire. Needless to say, the elves would do anything to avoid losing their dog.

Also of course, the gnomes would do anything they could to make the elves do just that. They had a giant gnome party every time it happened. A giant festival of evil and corruption, like River City Roundup, because they knew what would come next.

The biggest problem? The elves, unfortunately, liked to party. Sometimes, under the influence of the gnomes no doubt, the elves partied way too hard. When they woke up, their dog was usually gone. Every time it happened they tore their clothes and cried out, swearing it would never happen again, but sometimes it just did.

That's why the making of Daedalus was an even bigger cause for celebration for the elves. The previous dog they'd lost only a year after making him. That meant they were without their incarnated totem spirit for 99 years until the night Daedalus was made. It was an incredibly black time, and the elves hadn't drunk a drop since.

But, the making of Daedalus was such a happy occasion, so

the elves celebrated. They got drunker than they'd ever been before. And, as you might expect, they awoke the next morning to find Daedalus was gone.

That was truly terrible. They'd only had one night of the power of their incarnated totem in 99 years and they were facing another hundred with no more. The elves weren't immortal, and that much time without the totem could tip the scales permanently. The gnomes might finally win, bringing about the darkest dark age mankind had ever known. Darkness that would never end.

Things weren't good for little Daedalus either. He may have been important, but he certainly had no idea. The elves got power from him; he had none on his own. He was helpless, a little dachshund puppy alone in the back alleys and trash-strewn streets of some unknown city far, far from New York and the elves.

Luckily for Daedalus, he was found by an animal shelter instead of something worse. Through a series of animal shelter exchange programs, Daedalus was moved from city to city. Finally, he found himself in the animal shelter downtown and found himself Thomas and me.

Now, you might be wondering why that terrible dark age I mentioned hasn't happened yet. Be patient, I'll tell you. It's because all was not lost for the elves. It wasn't a problem if they lost their dog, just if they lost him and couldn't get him back.

See, the elves could track Daedalus. Believe me, they did nothing else once they realized they had lost him. They could track him through all those cities he'd been in until they found him and got him back.

But, the elves could only track their dog so far before the trail went cold. If the dog didn't eventually stop in one spot and stay there, the elves would get lost and never find him. That's when the gnomes would win. That's when the darkness would come.

So you see, I couldn't give up Daedalus. If I did then maybe the elves would never come back and find him. One more move might have been one move too many, and the darkness would swallow us all. There's no way I could live with myself if I let that happen. I just couldn't.

TUESDAY

Breakfast

Kate and Thomas were napping. Thomas had leaned against the wall and kicked his feet over the seat. Kate lay on top of him, leaning on his chest. They were both asleep and had been so for quite some time. That left me with very little to do.

As I mentioned before, I didn't need to sleep. They slept once in a while, but I don't think they needed to. I sure didn't. It seemed like they just did it for something to do. Been awake for a while? Bored of it? Might as well sleep for a bit then, for the illusion of variety. Experience a change of scenery, even if the scenery didn't really change.

It wasn't that we didn't need to sleep; we didn't seem to need to do a lot of things you might think we'd need to. I didn't understand why, but that was the way things were. We didn't need to wash; we just never became oily and never started to smell any worse no matter how long we'd been there. Our nails and hair never grew, which I thought was always supposed to go on, even after death. We didn't need to visit the doctor or dentist. We didn't need to work. We didn't need to invest in our company 401K. There were so many things we didn't need to do.

As for me, it wasn't so bad that I didn't need to sleep, except that I couldn't. I tried, but no luck. Sometimes I really wanted to pass out for a few hours, escape, but I couldn't seem to manage it.

I drank some of my coffee.

A mid-30s guy and his wife, I assumed, sat down at a table near our booth and started going through a menu.

The guy was blond with that most tasteless of all haircuts, the middle part. Round that out with a tucked-in blue Polo shirt and cheap black cloth slacks and he obviously worked in IT.

His wife wasn't much better. She had one of those asymmetrical hairstyles, shorter on one side with an even longer flip on part of the bangs of the shorter side, very obviously dyed ash blond.

Her skin-tone suggested her actual color was brunette. Worse, she had a loose denim skirt paired with a fake-denim cotton blouse. Denim on faux denim didn't suggest any possible occupation, though I was sure I could rule out fashion designer.

I admit it; I was staring. It wasn't polite, but that didn't bother me. What else was I going to do? For the moment they were the best show in town, and that meant they got stared at. Sorry.

What surprised me was realizing I wasn't the only one staring at them. Joining in my in-no-way-subtle stakeout was a red haired woman sitting alone in a booth close by. She hadn't noticed that I was watching as well, or that I was also watching her, and she made no attempt to hide what she was doing.

I guessed Redhead was about the same age as the man's wife, Mrs. Denim on Faux Denim (whom I'll Call Mrs. Faux Denim for short). Redhead, though, had a much better hairstyle, and by that I mean no style. It was just long and cascaded naturally, shining where the sun hit it. I also approved of her thin peasant dress, sort of a floral print with nice muted tones. Very understated. She probably worked the reference desk at some college library.

A waitress came over to take Mr. IT and Mrs. Faux Denim's order so they didn't notice Redhead or me watching. Looking carefully, though, I noticed Redhead wasn't an interested yet dispassionate observer like me. There was a mournful expression in her eyes, a yearning. She watched with an absent kind of pain. Clearly, Redhead was Mr. IT's former lover. They'd been together for so long, though that was in the past, and Mr. IT didn't even acknowledge her. He just went right on ordering. Oblivious.

They'd met while she was working in a coffee shop back when she was about 18. She was behind the counter and he'd come in with a date. That was okay, though. Redhead and Mr. IT didn't know each other yet. He couldn't be blamed for that one.

His date was a real social climber, though. That wasn't all right. Mr. IT just ordered a drip coffee, but Social Climber ordered a macchiato. A real one, Italian style, pure espresso with a couple dollops of foam. The drink was fine, but it was the fact that Social Climber didn't even like it that was the problem. She only drank it to seem sophisticated. Impress people, and not even just Mr. IT.

Social Climber was a frightening person, really one of the worst sorts of phony. Still, Mr. IT couldn't be blamed for that either. He hadn't even met Social Climber before that day. It was a blind date and he hadn't had a chance yet to see through her, so don't think too badly of him just because of his date.

Redhead could tell right away, though. The moment Social Climber walked into the shop, Redhead started grinding her teeth. It wasn't even something she thought about, not consciously. Her body and brain started acting on their own. It was as if Social Climber was sending her private psychic messages, aggressive invisible signals that called Redhead a skank and smacked her in the face. Everything Social Climber did, innocent or not, made it worse. Redhead became angrier and angrier the longer Social Climber was in the coffee shop.

Mind you, Redhead wasn't an angry type of person. She meditated once in a while, burned patchouli and sage bundles in her new apartment. Sometimes she forgot, but most of the time she tried to make visualizing healing and peaceful balls of blue energy part of her daily life. She gave money to homeless people and tried not to step on more worms when it rained than absolutely necessary, though that would have been gross anyway.

And she wasn't angry that day either. Nobody else that day put her on edge. In fact, she thought Mr. IT was even kind of cute. She might have flirted with him if he'd been alone.

But not Social Climber. Her she had hated instantly, as if recognizing an ancestral enemy. Like a mongoose first sighting a snake, or fire coming across water when it never had before, or ducks landing at the same pond as geese, a line was drawn in imaginary sand before a word was uttered. The macchiato hadn't started it; that was merely a shot in the ongoing battle.

Worse, the little priss just marched over to a table by the window after ordering, as if she expected Redhead to bring her drink over when it was ready. It wasn't that kind of coffee shop and everyone knew it. Customers carried their own drinks, even the ones who thought they were too good for that.

The little show really wasn't fair to Mr. IT either. She just acted as if he was going to pay, which had certainly not been discussed. It wasn't that kind of date yet. He probably would have offered to pay anyway, in hopes of making it that kind of date. But assuming like that took away his ability to make the gesture in favor of feeding Social Climber's massive ego.

Of course, Redhead didn't know that part because she'd never even seen Mr. IT before, much less talked to him, so that wasn't really part of what made her mad. The hand and foot service expectation, though, that was a real spit in the eye.

Still, Redhead restrained herself. Social climber may have been virtually begging to get taken down a peg, but Redhead had dealt with rude customers before. She wasn't new at the shop. She just tried to calm herself and think about those peaceful blue balls of energy, exploding and burning peaceful blue balls of energy.

Luckily, Mr. IT grabbed Social Climber's drink when it was done and brought it to the table. He'd waited like everyone else instead of sitting down, avoiding the confrontation that would surely have occurred when the finished drinks had sat, abandoned to their fate, on the counter. Redhead would not have brought them over.

Technically, Social Climber did nothing active to intentionally antagonize Redhead; Redhead knew this. Social Climber was just pretentious in her order, rude in walking off, and ignorantly arrogant while talking to Mr. IT about things designed to make her look superior to anyone in audio distance. None of that was specifically directed at Redhead. Social Climber was only being—obnoxious and appallingly abrasive though that was—herself.

Redhead understood this, as I said, but it did not help much. She seethed. She fumed. She raged. She wanted nothing more than to storm over and rip the hair out of Social Climber's idiot head.

I'm sure you'd have been able to sympathize if you could have heard the sort of things Social Climber said. I mean, who talks about cheese on a first date? How Gruyere is really superior to

Manchego because it has a more subtle flavor? It doesn't even make any sense! Believe me, the bitch really needed to die.

Mr. IT was being polite. It didn't look like he had any idea where the cheese thing even came from. He didn't know cheese, which shouldn't count against him even though cheese is very good, except for Kraft, and they hadn't even mentioned cheese before. Smiling and listening anyway, he appeared a little confused. He would have probably ignored it, though, in hopes of getting laid eventually.

What finally drove Redhead over the edge was Tolstoy. Isn't it always one of the Russians that do something like that? Turgenev, Pushkin, Bulgakov, Gogol, the Russians inspire such fierce passion, violence at its most pure. Surely Redhead could be excused for this fact alone.

Still, strange that it would be Tolstoy out of all the possible Russians that would spur fury. Wasn't he the man of peace? Wasn't he the gentle soul? Well, wasn't that at least what he was in his mind regardless of anything else?

"Really," Social Climber chirped, "I don't think anything important has been written since Tolstoy. Everyone should ignore anything since then and just read him if they read at all. Anything else is just a waste of time."

Redhead boiled. She loved Anna Karenina, but she was sure that Social Climber had never read any Tolstoy. Not even Resurrection. How dare she talk about Tolstoy to flaunt supposed good taste that she didn't even have? Redhead wanted to grab her in a headlock and not let go until she either read something or stopped struggling.

"And think of his dedication," Social Climber babbled on. Mr. IT, who probably struggled getting through Hawthorne much less Tolstoy, nodded politely. "Spending all those nights by candle, writing Crime and Punishment, never knowing if the name Tolstoy would be remembered."

That was when Redhead broke. She ran over to the table and pounded her fists upon it screaming, "Dostoyevsky wrote Crime and Punishment you fake little twit!" right into Social Climber's shocked and indignant face.

Redhead had hematite bracelets all up and down her arms because the coffee shop allowed jewelry though it required a uniform. The bracelets shattered and exploded as she pounded, covering Social Climber and Mr. IT in silver-ish dust and rock chips. It was beautiful in a way.

It probably goes without saying that Redhead was immediately fired. Social Climber got right up and found the manager, assuaging the slight to her all-important dignity through outrage. She didn't even make an attempt to appear concerned about the date. The insult and demand for prompt rectification were the primary concerns.

So, Redhead found herself escorted out the back door by the manager. Her employee badge was confiscated. Promises were made about a mailed check and stipulations were made that a reference could not ever be requested. None of that was a surprise.

However, Mr. IT was waiting outside by his car, which was a surprise. In fact, he had ditched Social Climber when she was too busy to notice. He actually apologized to Redhead and asked if she needed a ride, smiling at her and flashing his puppy dog eyes.

What could she do? She took him home.

Lunch

Kate and Thomas continued to sleep while Redhead and I continued to watch Mr. IT and Mrs. Faux Denim, though I also watched Redhead. Mr. IT and Mrs. Faux Denim's food had arrived and they were eating. Mr. IT had gone for a club sandwich and Mrs. Faux Denim had apparently made the bold choice of a Cobb salad.

And Redhead continued to watch Mr. IT and Mrs. Faux Denim, make no mistake about that. She couldn't have been as bored as I was, but she kept watching. She made no attempt to hide it, but no one other than me showed any apparent interest.

Mr. IT and Mrs. Faux Denim chewed their cud like dairy cows, absorbed. They didn't even talk to each other as they ate; though neither one seemed uncomfortable.

I couldn't believe that Mrs. Faux Denim didn't notice Redhead at all either. She didn't say hello, give a wave, or even act like she had seen her. I wondered if the slight was intentional, whether she was ignoring her or just being completely oblivious. There had to be an explanation. She'd known Redhead since they both started college.

There had been a mandatory orientation for freshman put on by the university. New students were required to attend, but the university was not required to make it useful. It was held in a huge auditorium. A faceless administrator droned on in the very front and possibly thousands of freshman filled the seats. Redhead sat somewhere near the back, as far back as possible while still finding a seat. She was there because she had to be and she had some small hope that something important would be said, though she didn't really expect it. That small hope faded further as the presentation wore on.

"You are not in high school anymore," the faceless voice chided. "At least, not if you are in the correct place." He chuckled at his own joke. A sympathetic but forced laugh made its way through the crowd. "You are adults now, and it is time to act like adults. You are in control of your own destinies now."

"Really?" Redhead mumbled to herself. "I can't imagine why I'm making myself suffer through this if it's really up to me. I must secretly hate myself and want to be punished."

"The university will be available to provide advice," the administrator continued, ignorant of Redhead's comment, "but it will be up to you to decide what to do with that advice. You decide your own path; we cannot do that for you. We can only help you along. The rest is all up to you."

"I generally stick to well-lit major streets," Redhead murmured.

"And that means you have to decide where you would like to go. There will not be anyone to force you anymore."

"At least there's that. Now I won't have to carry my rape whistle."

"If you do not desire to do well, you will not. If you desire to do well, then you will. Life will be as simple as that. You will have the materials you need and it will be your choice. You will receive all the credit for your success, but you will have to do all the work. We are merely the tools; it is you who are the craftsmen."

We can agree on the tool part. Redhead thought—but a voice next to her murmured it out loud.

She looked over and saw Mrs. Faux Denim, though she wasn't married back then. She also wasn't wearing denim. Mrs. Faux Denim realized she'd been overheard, but didn't seem embarrassed. She smirked instead, perhaps sensing a sympathetic spirit.

"You are only limited by the strength of your character," the voice continued blathering from the front of the hall. "Now is your opportunity to find out what that character is. I am reminded of the words of Alice Hamilton, who, at the age of 87, once said—"

"Where's my teeth?" Redhead interrupted, quiet but deliberately loud enough for Mrs. Faux Denim to overhear.

Mrs. Faux Denim laughed. Several nearby students turned.

She glared at them until they turned back. Redhead smiled and Mrs. Faux Denim gave her a wry smile in return.

"If you want to succeed, do the work. Study," the far-off administrator advised. "If you do not need to go to class then you do not need to take the course. You might be able to pass by opening a book a week before the final. People have done that. However, you will not learn what you will need to know for later life because you will forget just as quickly."

"I'll never learn," Mrs. Faux Denim mumbled, loud enough for Redhead to hear, and pretended to reluctantly shake her head. "It's sad."

"As sad as having to be here?" Redhead asked her, whispering.

"I don't think quite that much," Mrs. Faux Denim whispered back. "I don't think anything could be that sad."

"Do you want to make good use of your time at this institution?" the man asked from the front. "Listen to your professors; they know more than you realize. Study before you come to class. That way, you will be able to ask questions. When you don't understand, speak up so you can find out."

"When you're hungry," Mrs. Faux Denim muttered, "eat. When you're tired, sleep. When you need air, breathe."

"When you're proposed to by your cousin the Reverend, hold out for the rich guy that can't stand your family," Redhead added.

"Students complain about the high price of education," the voice droned, "but the cost of misusing an education is far, far higher. To pay and have nothing to show is the worst fate. Keep this in mind during your time here. It will serve you well."

"I'd complain more about having to sit here," Redhead whispered.

"No doubt. I'll be sure to keep that in mind during my time here," Mrs. Faux Denim replied.

Redhead looked around at the other students. Their attention was rapt, as if there was actually something earthshaking being said, as if their eventual degrees would only count if they listened to that speech. Her and Mrs. Faux Denim appeared to be the only ones that did not want to be there.

"Why are we here anyway?"

"It was required," Redhead reminded.

Mrs. Faux Denim considered this. "They did a sign-in sheet at the door. I signed, did you?"

"Of course."

"You think they're planning to do it again on the way out?" She smirked. "Or do you think they'd never know if we got the hell out?"

Redhead looked around. They were in the middle of a row, students in front and back as well as to both sides. "Depends if we could do it without getting noticed," she responded. "It would be too easy to stop us if we just tried to get up and slip out."

"You're saying the more we tried to hide, the more we'd be seen?"

"Yep." She looked up toward the front and then back to Mrs. Faux Denim. "So, how do we do it?"

Mrs. Faux Denim crossed her arms and leaned back in her brown metal folding chair. "I came up with the plan to get out. You have to figure out how. It's only fair, surprise me."

Redhead smiled. Fair or not, it was certainly more entertaining than listening to the speech. Tapping her foot, she contemplated possible plans. She needed something fun.

Clutching a hand to her mouth suddenly, she lurched her body forward. She filled her cheeks with air and then pretended to swallow. She did it again. Mrs. Faux Denim looked at her, curious. A few other students looked as well.

Suddenly, Redhead leapt to her feet. Her metal folding chair fell with a clatter. More students looked toward her and the voice at the front paused in the middle of a sentence. She lurched forward again, holding her mouth hard with her hand.

Mrs. Faux Denim stood up quickly and put an arm around Redhead's shoulder. "Make way! She's going to be sick!"

They both charged for the door. Students scattered, making a clear path. A few didn't appear to be moving quickly enough, but a few more fake heaves from Redhead sped them up. Others even helped them along, pushing them both gently but insistently toward the door. No one tried to stop them before they made it out.

"Yes . . . well . . . as I was saying—" the voice continued before they shut the door to the hall behind them, cutting off the sound of the lecture.

"Nice choice," Mrs. Faux Denim complimented. "Vomit. Very effective."

"Thanks," Redhead replied as they walked down the empty hallway. "I usually can't fake throwing up, but sitting in there made me feel enough like it that I didn't have too much trouble. If we hadn't gotten out, I probably would have done it for real."

"I'm glad we got out then," Mrs. Faux Denim quipped. "These shoes are new."

"I would've tried to keep it on someone who'd been paying attention. They would have deserved it."

After they'd walked for a moment Mrs. Faux Denim stopped and turned toward Redhead. "I think I deserve a drink after having sat though as much of that as I did. How about you?"

Redhead shrugged. "Minor."

"Me, too." She put an arm around Redhead's shoulder and started walking her. "Tell you what, I know a dive bar just off campus where the bartenders forget to check IDs if you undo enough buttons. A few more and they forget to charge. You game?"

"Sounds good."

"Super! Then let's get started on your real freshman orientation. Remember this, unless we manage to drink so much that we can't. It will serve you well during your time here."

Redhead smiled. She fell into step with Mrs. Faux Denim and they marched out of the moldy smelling building, out into the warm sunlight.

Dinner

I thought about waking Kate and Thomas. They'd been sleeping long enough, and it wasn't like they were really tired. All I had to do was make a loud noise on the table or something like that. Still, I let them keep sleeping a little longer. I was sure they'd be awake soon enough.

Over at the watched table, Mr. IT and Mrs. Faux Denim were still sitting. They'd finished eating and their waitress had cleared their dishes, but they hadn't left. I guessed they were waiting for dessert, probably pie.

Redhead hadn't left either, though she wasn't watching anymore. She just sat drinking iced tea with two packets of sweetener, staring out the window. I never noticed a waitress go over, but she never seemed to run out of iced tea. She must have been taking tiny little sips. Maybe she didn't want to leave before Mr. IT and Mrs. Faux Denim.

After all, things couldn't have gone on the way I'd told you. Otherwise, things would have been very different right then. They wouldn't have been at separate tables, for one thing. It would have been Redhead at the table with Mr. IT, or with Mrs. Faux Denim. There would have been no nearby booth. Or, maybe all three of them would have been at the same table, but Mr. IT and Mrs. Faux Denim wouldn't have been together alone. Certainly not married.

Maybe they wouldn't have been in a Village Inn at all. Maybe they would have been at a fancy place, or at home having a barbecue or some such thing. They could have even been out in a park having a picnic; it looked like nice weather outside the window. Not that there is anything wrong with a Village Inn, mind you, but if things had been different then they would have been different.

But, things hadn't been different for a long time. Redhead had just kind of added Mr. IT to her life after that time she took him home. At first, he just never left. For one reason or another, he kept staying the night. Finally, she moved him in, absorbed him. She was Redhead with a supplemental Mr. IT.

It was convenient. He chipped in money for rent after he let his old place go and he washed dishes and such. When she wanted to go to dinner with somebody, he was already there. If she wanted to have sex, she didn't have to find a partner. The arrangement was satisfactory in all respects.

And the situation went on for a long time, years. She saw no reason why it couldn't go on many years more, perhaps however many years there were left. It wasn't like they were using anything up. There was nothing to run out; they just worked well together and were pleasantly happy.

Except that at a certain point, Mr. IT didn't seem to be so pleasantly happy anymore. There was something he wanted that he couldn't articulate, something she apparently didn't have. All of a sudden, he had complaints.

It seemed like he was upset that they hadn't magically fused into a single person. Maybe he thought if they lived together long enough they would start to merge, eventually unable to tell where one ended and the other began. He started wondering aloud where they were going, but Redhead didn't understand why. She was perfectly content to stay right where she was.

He actually became upset one night that none of their friends had ever given them a couple name. You know, some combination of their names used as an easy reference since so often if you referred to one of the couple you needed to refer to the other. Mr. I-head was one possibility he suggested friends might have taken to calling them. Red-T was another. He was showing that friends could have, but never had.

For some reason, he seemed to think she wasn't really with him, though they were certainly together. Frankly, she didn't see how they could be any more together. She even told him that. What did he want? Wearing the same underpants at the same time? Neither of them had underwear big enough for that.

But, he insisted she wasn't really involved with him on any

real level, not engaged. He was additional, but not an integral part of her life. He was no different than her favorite fire opal earrings or her knitted rainbow scarf. An accessory. They were living lives together, but not building a life together.

She didn't pay a great deal of attention. They were fine. Besides, what could she do? She wasn't sure what he really wanted.

Sure, she didn't think much of some of the things he really got into. She didn't want to go to LAN parties with his friends. Why would she? The girlfriends all sat and watched TV while the guys played; there was no function to having her there.

And she hadn't gone to the banquet when he'd gotten that network certification award. What of it? He'd always told her what a joke that one was. She didn't think it was a big deal to miss.

Besides, she didn't make him do things in her life he wouldn't have wanted to do either. Wasn't that fair then? She hadn't made him sit through her graduation, or go to her grandma Nadia's funeral. It wasn't a problem; they just did separate things sometimes. That was healthy.

Or, maybe it was a problem because eventually he got his own place. Then he came over less and less until he stopped seeing her at all. His stuff was all gone and his name was off the Internet bill. He didn't even have any of his off-brand energy drinks in her fridge.

She should have done something, but work was really busy right then. Besides, she was upset he'd gone that far just to prove his point. Surely he'd miss her and come to his senses eventually. Then things could go on as before . . . except they didn't.

Mrs. Faux Denim started vanishing as well about the same time. At first they hung out most of the time. Bars, concerts, lunches, coffee. Since Mr. IT wasn't around, Redhead had a lot of time. It was like The Mary Tyler Moore Show, but without all the rapid costume changes.

But then that all changed as well. Mrs. Faux Denim started to be busy some nights. Only a few at first, but the number increased over time. Sometimes she didn't feel like leaving the house and stayed in, ignoring her phone. Surely Redhead understood.

And Redhead did. Obviously. They weren't dating or anything. If Mrs. Faux Denim had other things to do or didn't feel like doing anything, then that was fine. It was cool when they hung out, but life didn't end when they didn't. Mrs. Faux Denim had her own life, after all.

Not that Redhead didn't, mind you. She wasn't trying to patch some hole that got kicked in one of her walls when Mr. IT took off. She had interests; she had things she could do. There was a lot of reading she'd been meaning to get done. She read a lot already, but had always intended to do more when there was time. Her great aunt had offered to teach her how to crochet. Perhaps she could even learn French.

But then Mrs. Faux Denim stopped hanging out with Redhead at all. That wasn't fine. The only time they talked was when Redhead called, and Mrs. Faux Denim didn't return messages. Eventually, she wouldn't even take Redhead's calls.

It was a bit of a mystery until Redhead found out Mr. IT and Mrs. Faux Denim had gotten together. Once that was clear, little further explanation was required or wanted. Redhead needed no further information when they moved in together, or even when they got married. She would, however, have liked to receive an invitation to the wedding. She wouldn't have gone, probably, but it would have been nice to be asked. She probably would have sent a toaster, a crappy two-slot one that didn't fit bagels.

That brings us to the present meal. Mr. IT and Mrs. Faux Denim at their table; Redhead in her booth. Redhead had finally run out of iced tea. Mr. IT and Mrs. Faux Denim? They were eating pie. Both had gone for chocolate silk.

Sides

Okay, obviously none of that stuff I've been talking about in the last chapter was really about Mr. IT, Mrs. Faux Denim, or Redhead. I'd never seen them before. Let's not get into what I was really talking about.

I've got something else I want to discuss, but I thought we should clear the air first. The air gets thick enough on its own sometimes without us having to make it any worse. It's a wonder we even understand each other at all.

What's got me more interested, though, was how unconcerned Thomas, Kate, and I seemed to be about our lives outside the Village Inn. I didn't even know if they'd thought about it at all like I had, though just a little at that, but we never talked about it.

I mean sure, we talked about Daedalus, but nothing beyond that. No jobs, homes, other people, or anything. Not really, not in a way that showed we were actually concerned. Surely, we should have been. Before we walked in the door that day, that was all we had. After that, all we had was pancakes.

Of course, our lives outside didn't matter much at that point. We were trapped. We didn't know if we'd ever go back, so why worry if there was anything to go back to? It made a certain amount of sense. And, even if we did get out someday, how long would it really have been? There was no way of being sure. Everyone and everything we'd known, besides the three of us, may well have been gone by that point.

I was definitely out of a job. There was no way around that. One no-call-no-show was cause for termination, and I was certain we'd been there for much, much longer than a single day. Years, maybe. Decades was more likely. The bookstore might not have been in business anymore. Heck, books could have been long gone by that point.

Even though I'd been fired, I probably could have talked my

way back in if I ever could have gotten out of the Village Inn and the bookstore was still there. I'd gotten away with a lot before. Corporate policy often necessitated firing, but nothing prevented the manager from hiring me back. He always did.

Kate was untouchable, of course, since she was her own boss. Unless she fired herself for absenteeism, she would have been fine. Her graphic art clients might have walked, if not sued, and she might have had to build things back up from scratch. Still, she was good at that.

Thomas was more uncertain. It all depended on whether or not anyone had noticed and how long we'd actually been trapped. He did remote tech support; people emailed him problems and he fixed in the background. Conceivably, people might have thought things got better after they emailed, since Thomas said most things that got reports weren't real problems. They might not have noticed that he didn't do anything. Or, one of the other techs might have taken care of things if it had been a real problem. Those emails went to the group at once and whoever got there first, fixed. It was possible Thomas still had a job and money kept getting automatically deposited in his bank account. Then again, maybe someone had noticed and Thomas had gotten sacked. It was tough to say.

There was also the question of our respective homes and other such things. Our clothes, our books or computers, our collections of toothpicks formerly used by rock celebrities, anything could have happened. Were strangers using our stuff? Living in our lives?

Thomas owned his and Kate's house at least. That would have been safe for a while, unless something like a fire or tornado had occurred. He'd bought it outright, going for a shit house to be able to do so, just so he wouldn't have a mortgage or anything like that to deal with. Because of that, there was no one to foreclose for missed payments, but what about taxes? At some point, even Thomas's house could have been gone.

My apartment was much more fragile. I mean, rent was due every month. Someone would surely notice if I'd been gone that long. What would they do if I were missing? My landlord had let things slide a month or two now and again if I buttered him up, but this was a different story altogether. Besides which, I wasn't there to do any buttering.

Mom had Daedalus, so she would have noticed right away that I hadn't come back for him. She would certainly have taken care of him at least. Would she have done the same thing for my apartment? She'd helped with rent before when I was short; would she handle it if I were gone for months? Or years? Take care of things? Would someone have taken care of Thomas and Kate's house the same way?

Or, even if they couldn't save our homes, would they clean up our messes and store our stuff? Moved us out and boxed our things into storage units to await our hopefully eventual safe return? Put our pictures on milk cartons?

There was no way to know. The best thing was to accept and let go.

And we pretty much had, which was weird. People never accept anything that is best for them to accept. They rant and rage in futile anger; that's just part of being human. Not us, though. We didn't seem to care one bit. We were calm and tranquil like sleeping housecats, well fed ones.

It's true, I did wonder once in a while. Still, that was more curiosity than anything, something to keep myself busy thinking. Even I wasn't really that concerned. Not really.

Beverages

I feel like I should really make up something about Thomas, Kate, or me here, or even a combination of the group of us, but I can't. It's not that I never made anything up about any of us, just that for some reason I never made up anything about us while we were at the Village Inn. At least, not that I remembered. It's kooky, but it's true.

Instead, I'm going to tell you something I made up about our waitress. You remember our waitress? Sherri? Remember how I said I'd share something later that I made up about her? Well, I wasn't lying. And, it's later now.

After all, she deserved the gift of a story. What with all the unending servitude, the no tip, the having to put up with our shenanigans, as well as everything we'd done and would do to her, we owed her something. She was one of the good ones, and she deserved better than the likes of us. I'm sure she would have preferred money, and possibly that we would leave at some point, but this is what she got.

You see, Sherri had a connection problem. It wasn't that she lacked social skills. She was certainly pleasant enough for us, and we were enough to try anyone's patience. No, Sherri had a different kind of connection problem.

The problem was that Sherri's skin had a peculiar magnetic polarization. In fact, her skin had the opposite polarization of any other living creature. You might not know that your skin is polarized, but trust me, it is. Every living creature gives off an electrical field. It's part of nature. And, that electrical field is magnetized, which of course means it has a polarization.

The reason this has never been noticed, other than the fact that these electrical fields are pretty weak, is that all living creatures have an identical polarization. Nobody notices because no one is different. It's just like skin color; nobody would notice skin color if there was only one to have.

Of course, it isn't really true that absolutely everybody's polarization was the same. As I said before, Sherri's was opposite. Exactly opposite, in fact, from the polarization radiated by every other living thing.

Keep in mind, though, that Sherri didn't know anything about this. Certainly don't tell her, since she doesn't know. It wouldn't help any. Believe me, I thought about telling her, but it was better that she didn't know.

I mean, how could she know? Nobody else even knew they had a polarization! How would Sherri be the only one who knew, and on top of that, know hers was opposite? That would be ridiculous.

It's all because of a certain lipid-producing enzyme in her skin. Hers has a defect that causes a reverse of the polarized electrical field that should be produced. And no one else has had an enzyme quite like hers, though they had a non-defective one that resulted in normal polarization. In truth, it was just a tiny little difference, a few atoms shifted here and there in a molecule. However, that tiny little difference made all the difference in the world.

You see, that polarization difference made for a real problem. To be specific, it made for a connection problem.

Have you ever held the opposite ends of two magnets together? When they're opposite polarities they attract, but when they're the same they repel. Right? No matter how hard you try, those same-sided magnets don't want to go together. Really weak ones you can kind of force for a bit, but they fight for all they're worth.

Now, I know what you're thinking. You're wrong, though. You're thinking that if her field was magnetized opposite everyone else's that she wouldn't be able to stop touching people, right? That every time she came close to somebody . . . smack! She couldn't help herself from latching right onto them. Maybe you're thinking that because of such, everyone thought Sherri was a slut. Am I right? Well, you're wrong.

I mean, think about it. What would the world be like if it really worked that way? I already told you everyone else was polarized the same. That would mean all the people in the world would repel when they tried to touch each other. Except Sherri. We all know that doesn't happen.

The weird thing was that it was Sherri's reverse polarization-field that repelled everyone else's. No one knew why, primarily because no scientist even knew this was out there to study.

For some reason, because everyone else's fields were the same, they passed right through each other. Like nothing was there, the fields I mean, not the people. It was almost like a filter, a field of one polarity screens out the field of the same polarity. Reverse polarities, though, meaning Sherri and any other living thing, didn't screen each other out. Instead, the fields contacted and stopped each other cold. It wasn't repulsion exactly, which wouldn't make much sense either I suppose since the fields were opposite polarities and should have attracted from everything we know about magnetics, but instead was more like solid contact. Like the fields were solid matter, which they weren't.

Okay, we're getting pretty complex here, but I can boil it down for you. The basic fact was that Sherri could never touch, never truly touch, the skin of another living being.

Sherri didn't know this, and neither did anyone else. Like I said before, those fields are pretty weak. Really, really weak. That doesn't mean they're not there, though, that there's no effect, just that they only extend a tiny distance from the surface of the skin. Too small for you to be able to see; the distance is microscopic. However, that distance was very important to Sherri.

Think, Sherri would go to touch somebody. Let's not make it complicated; just say she went to touch somebody's hand. Micrometers or picometers from the other person's hand, Sherri's field would contact the other person's field. Like a truck hitting a concrete bridge abutment, all forward motion would stop. Contact would be made, but no skin touch would occur.

Sure, it may have looked like they were touching; the distance would be too small to see. But, they wouldn't be. Not even a little bit. It's like a light switch; it's either on or off. Either Sherri would be touching someone or she wouldn't be, and she wouldn't be.

Believe me, she couldn't.

So, it would look like Sherri was touching the other person. It would even feel like it to both. Their hands would be touching something, the fields that wouldn't let them pass as opposed to skin. It's just the skin that wouldn't touch. They would even feel warmth, since their hands would be close enough to feel each other's body heat. Still, though they wouldn't know it, there'd be no actual touching.

That's why I say Sherri has a connection problem. You might not think it would be a big problem, but it's not a problem you've ever had. Connection is the most important thing there is; connection is vital.

Sherri's problem was actually inherited, even though no one else had ever had her problem. A particular chromosome produced the enzyme, one that Sherri's family had been carrying around for over 5000 years. It's just that for everyone else in Sherri's family, the gene was recessive. Only in Sherri did the gene ever activate.

So it was actually cosmically funny in a way, even though it really wasn't funny at all. I mean, genes are passed on as a result of touching, contact and mating. However, 5000 years of that kind of touching left Sherri unable to touch. I guess funny is the wrong word to use, but it's something like that. It's something far more horrible and sad, whatever the word is for a far more horrible and sad version of cosmically funny.

And think about what this actually meant for Sherri, to never know the truth of her skin contacting the skin of another human being. To never know that touch and to never know that she didn't know. She was alone in a way no one else had ever been alone.

Remember that DUI problem-boyfriend I decided she had? Sure, she'd been intimate with him, but never as intimate as other people could be, never as intimate as she thought she was being. Never had the reassurance of skin, neither with him nor with any other person she'd been intimate with. She tried, and tried very hard, but it never quite worked.

Worse, she knew on some level that something was wrong.

She just didn't know what that something was. Never having had human touch, her soul craved it. She felt desperately and tragically alone. She felt a burning need for that connection, even though she had no idea what it was. It was simply a biological instinct, not rational, not articulable, and not understandable.

It caused her to cling, without being able to touch. As a result, she drove people away. People flee desperation. In turn, this made Sherri shut down, afraid of everyone leaving her, afraid to show her need. It was indeed a complete isolation.

The most tragic part is that it was easily correctible if only she knew what the problem was. A corrective enzyme could have been applied topically to her skin, such as in a fat or lotion, which would have then corrected her defective enzyme. That would have caused her electrical field to re-polarize, to become the same as everyone else's. She would have been able to touch the skin of another person for the first time. For real.

However, though this was within the power of modern science to accomplish, no one had ever realized the need. Probably, no one ever will. Because no one knew Sherri could not touch, no scientist ever designed an assay to detect Sherri's defective enzyme. And, because no one knew about the defective enzyme, no one would ever develop a corrective to help her.

I really felt bad for Sherri. I felt bad for her connection problem, and I felt bad for thinking it up for her. What could I do, though? It's just what I thought of as I sat in that booth. I felt awful, but there was nothing I could do.

WEDNESDAY

Breakfast

Thomas shuffled the cards. You remember the cards, right? The ones he and Kate were playing with a while back? Well, Thomas shuffled them. Nobody was playing a game; he was just shuffling.

I sat on my side of the booth and Thomas on his. Kate was in the bathroom. She'd been in there for quite a while. I don't even think she had to go. I think she was just in there. That was fine, though. Thomas and I could hang for a while.

"Let's play a game," I suggested. "Hand me the deck."

Shrugging, he handed the cards over. "I'm game," he said. "What'll we play?"

"Armistice," I told him, starting to deal. I dealt the whole deck, half in a pile to him and half in a pile to me. Then I tidied up each so we both had a nice, neat little stack.

"Armistice?" His eyebrows rose. "Never heard of it."

"Just made it up. It's like war, but completely different."

"Okay then." He laughed. "I guess I know how to play then, except that I don't have a clue."

I smiled, taking a drink of my coffee. I'd actually thought up the idea while watching him shuffle. I hadn't thought out all the rules yet. Really, I wasn't sure the game would totally work. It seemed like an interesting idea, though, and it wasn't like either of us had anything better to do.

"So," he went on when he realized I wasn't going to start explaining, "are you planning on telling me how to play? Or, is that your winning strategy, keeping me in the dark?"

"It's simple." I shrugged. "I'll tell you as we play."

"If you say so." He reached for a card.

"No! Don't do anything until I tell you."

He laughed again and pulled back his hand. "This could get difficult. Are you sure you don't want to tell me the rules first?"

"Look," I told him, "some of it will be simpler if I tell you when things come up. For now, though, we have to decide who is going first. Each run through the cards you have is one round and the same person goes first for the whole round."

"Ah, I see. Should I go first then?"

"It doesn't matter," I said. "As long as we're consistent. That's the important part. You draw a card first this time and we'll alternate on the next round. You have to alternate; that's how it works."

Thomas looked at me. He had a half-smile on his face. I wondered if he knew I was making this up as I went along. Either that, or he thought I was conning him to win easily. As if I needed to; Thomas was terrible at cards.

"All right," he sighed, drawing a card. He set it down on the table. Jack of spades. He looked up at me, waiting.

I drew a card and set it next to his. We both looked. Five of hearts. I wasn't worried, though. I'd at least figured out this much of the game.

"Let me guess, you win, right? It's the opposite of war and the high card loses?"

"Don't be ridiculous." I shook my head. "That one's a draw."

"What? What's the point here anyway? One card is clearly higher than the other; someone's got to win."

"Nope," I insisted. "Not in armistice. One card was higher than the other so the throw was a draw. We toss both in a discard pile and go onto the next throw."

Thomas tapped a finger on the table. "So, what happens when we run out of cards? Seems like that could happen pretty quick."

"I told you, that's the end of a round. Then we re-shuffle and split the cards again. In the next round, I'll go first. It's fun, you'll see."

"I'm not sure I see the fun if nobody can win. Do you play forever, or until someone gives up?"

I rolled my eyes at him, deliberately for effect. I was having more fun stringing him along than I was playing the game. That probably wasn't a good sign for the game itself, but games weren't the only possible source of amusement. This was fine, too.

"I didn't say nobody could win, just that this particular throw was a draw."

"Explain," Thomas challenged.

"Okay, I responded, thinking quickly. "The point is that war as a game operates under a basic flawed assumption. This game corrects that assumption. As a result, it's a better game."

"And what is that flawed assumption?"

"Well . . . each throw of war is supposed to represent a battle. Right? Whoever draws the higher card supposedly brings more force. Thus, they win for that card. It's the simplest war game, a basic battle of attrition and nothing more."

"Right," Thomas agreed. "So where's the flaw?"

"It doesn't reflect how things really are. Sure, the party that has more troops generally wins a battle. However, the battle is only a small part of the big picture."

"I see. It's only part of the war. But, isn't war made up of a bunch of different battles? It's simplified, but it works."

"Only if you see war as the big picture," I countered. "War already does that. But, that's where the flaw is."

"Really." Thomas smiled. "And what is the big picture then?"

"Everything! Everybody in all the countries, the ones fighting and the ones that stayed at home. Even the countries that aren't in the war are part of it. The big picture is everything in the whole world."

"And this is somehow fixed by the higher card not winning the battle? Or, the lower for that matter?"

"Battles have costs," I explained. "Even the winner of a battle is a loser in some way, at least most of the time. Acting like you've won if you've drawn a higher or lower card ignores the costs of the battle itself. Winning in that context isn't really winning."

Thomas groaned, holding one hand over his face. "We're back to no way to win! Am I just supposed to refuse to play?"

"That isn't how it works either," I replied. "Just draw."

Thomas drew a six next and I drew a ten. I set the cards in the discard pile and motioned for him to draw again. Finally, about ten draws later, we both drew fives.

"Armistice!" I clapped. "My point!"

"Wait . . . what?"

"I told you, winning a battle isn't really winning. The only way for two warring countries to win anything is to have an armistice, to stop fighting, and nobody does that unless the battle is going to be a draw. If anyone thought they could win, they'd fight. It's only when we draw exactly the same card that we can have an armistice."

"So, why is it your point?"

"Because you're going first this round," I explained. "You were the aggressor and I drew the card that resulted in the cessation of fighting. Therefore, I win one point. You can get points on the rounds I go first."

Thomas smiled. "I guess that's actually fair."

"Here, we can keep track of points using the sweetener packets since we don't have a pen." I grabbed a packet from the little metal thing on the table that held the pie menu. I set it on my side of the discard pile.

"So, whoever gets the most points wins?" Thomas asked. "Do we play to a certain number, or do we just quit when we get sick of it? Seems like nobody would want to quit while they were behind; they'd just want to wait until they were ahead again. It still makes it kind of antagonistic."

I cursed silently. I hadn't gotten that far. He was right. I needed something that would end the game, something not open to argument. Argument ran counter to the point of the game.

"Simple," I said, suddenly thinking of an idea. "The first to get to eleven points wins. Armistice Day is the eleventh of November."

Thomas laughed again, shaking his head. "You know," he said quietly after a moment, "I really missed the fun we used to have."

Lunch

Kate was still in the bathroom after we finished playing Armistice. Again, I don't think she was actually using the bathroom. I think she wanted a little time alone. Really, the bathroom was the only place to get that inside the Village Inn.

I understood her, too, I really did. All we did was sit there, the three of us, apparently endlessly. She and Thomas at least slept once in a while for a change, but that still had the three of us sitting together. No time apart at all. I didn't mind, for some reason, but I could see how it could drive her up a wall.

Actually, it seemed pretty terrible to have to resort to the bathroom in order to get away. The Village Inn kept it as clean and nice-smelling as anyone could, but it was still a bathroom. Toilets aren't exactly comfortable chairs for any length of time. Besides, you didn't always get to be alone in there. Other people had to really use the bathroom, and that wasn't likely to be a pleasant thing to have to sit through. You had to hear it, even if you didn't have to see it.

Thomas and I didn't discuss Kate's absence. I don't think he knew what she was doing, or he was at least being a gentleman and not discussing what he thought she was doing. Either way, if Kate wanted to hang out in the bathroom, we let her.

Thomas was lying down on his seat. His head was at the very end, by the aisle, and his feet were propped up on the wall. He wasn't sleeping; he was just lying there. I was facing the opposite way on my seat, leaned up against the wall. I had my knees bent and my feet on the seat. We looked like kids hanging out in front of a drugstore.

Our waitress had been by several times while we sat like that. She didn't stop and ask us if we needed anything. Instead, she'd walk nearby and look at us. I guess she figured that would save her some time. If we wanted something we could have flagged her down. Otherwise, she wasted little time or breath while still taking care of us. It was actually an ingenious little system, quite efficient and all.

"What was your favorite vacation?" Thomas asked, still reclined on the seat. "What was the one you liked best?"

I turned to look at him, though I couldn't really see his face under the table. "Are we playing another game? I don't remember you coming up with games."

"Sure, if you want." He paused. "Well, I suppose it's not really a game, more of a question. I don't want you to create something. I just want to know."

"Okay," I said, thinking about the question. "Which one would I pick?"

"No," Thomas instructed. "You'll justify it if you have to think. I want to know the real answer, the one before any high-level thought muddles things up. Just say the first one that pops into your head as your favorite vacation."

"Okay, the trip my mom and I took to the Grand Canyon."

He shifted in his seat. "Tell me about it."

It wasn't a 'real' question. We were escaping, as much as we could, given the fact that it was impossible to leave. In fact, because we couldn't physically leave, we probably needed mental escape even more. I guessed this was what Thomas had come up with, the best that he thought he could do.

I mean, what is a vacation if not an escape? Sure, it's supposed to be fun, depending what kind of vacations you take. Still, vacations are supposed to be escapes from the routine of normal life. That's why we take them, so we don't crack under the strain quite as soon.

And, if you can't take an actual vacation, such as if you are stuck inside a Village Inn for all eternity, why not take a mental vacation? Such as by reminiscing about an actual vacation. It may not be comparable to actually getting away, and don't believe any liar who says it is, but you might as well if it's all you've got. Something is better than nothing, or at least it seems that way.

"It was actually more than just the Grand Canyon. We took

two weeks and drove all over the Southwest. The Grand Canyon, Four Corners, L.A., Disneyland, Universal Studios, San Francisco, we went all over the place. I guess it must have been more than just the Southwest, too, because we did Rushmore and Yosemite. Sometimes we camped and sometimes we stayed in hotels; we did whatever we felt like."

"Sounds nice," Thomas commented.

"It was," I agreed. "I was seven and my mom got a chunk of money after the divorce was final and my dad took off to Cleveland. I guess she needed a break. So, we started driving."

"Did you camp in a tent?" Thomas asked.

"Sort of. We drove around in my mom's old wood-paneled station wagon and towed this green wooden camper trailer behind us. It was flat, like a truck bed, but when you turned a crank, a tent popped out. If we felt like it, we cranked and camped. If not, we found a cheap hotel."

"Did you take a lot of pictures?"

"Well, sort of on that, too. We took pictures everywhere, hundreds, but we didn't bring back a whole lot. My mom kept taking the camera out of the car to snap something at overlooks and places like that and then she'd forget the camera on the roof when we drove off. We must have lost 20 cameras that way. I guess she had a lot on her mind."

"So, why was that your favorite trip?" Thomas asked.

I hesitated. It felt like Thomas was driving at something with all of this, and that was unusual. Thomas didn't do guile real well. Still, I couldn't be sure if his agenda was hostile or not. Maybe he wanted to make a point about something and was taking his sweet time getting to it.

In the end, I decided to play along. After all, it wasn't like I didn't have time to spare. I could let him be as obtuse as he wanted to be.

"I don't know," I replied slowly. "There was something about it that always struck me. My mom and me, wandering around aimlessly like nomads, it was exciting. There seemed to be all these little things, a granite rock shaped like an arrow I found at

Yellowstone, a rough leather keychain from Rushmore, the musty smell of the canvas tent of the camper, the lobster we split at Fisherman's Wharf, standing in four states at the same time holding hands, things like that. It makes me really happy for some reason when I think about it."

"Good answer," Thomas replied.

"Thanks. What's yours?"

"Our trip to Daytona," he said. He didn't pause at all. He must have been thinking about it the entire time. Heck, if he wanted to talk about that trip, he should have just talked.

"I remember that trip." To show I remembered, I grimaced. Part was for show, but part was from remembering.

"You found that hotel deal and we happened to have a long weekend, so we got in the car and left. It was so trusting, driving off like that. My car wouldn't even go in reverse, since we hadn't scraped up enough for the new transmission, or a new car, yet."

"I remember. I was the one who had to push us backwards out of every parking spot," I muttered.

"Since the car was pretty much fragged anyway, you glued rubber ducks all over it. I can't even remember why . . . but you did it."

"I had some ducks," I said, "and some glue."

"And you hung a Daytona or Bust sign in the back window, white poster board and black magic marker. To be honest, the way that Metro was, I was pretty sure it was going to be bust."

"You'll excuse me if I don't get all nostalgic for that one," I quipped. "There were a few rough spots. The sunburn so bad I needed Prednisone, the fact that the deal hotel was under major construction, trying to sleep overnight in a black car at a rest stop in Georgia in summertime. It wasn't exactly a smooth vacation.

"But there were good spots," he countered. "Don't forget stopping by the steak buffet when all those aging bikers took their top-enhanced old ladies, tubing down the river alone through that cypress forest, standing in the water and letting it pull us across sand that felt as hard as cement, going nude at Apollo Beach, or things like that. It was a hell of a trip."

"I'll take your word for it."

"It was," he argued. "I still have that shark in a bottle we got, and that cheap souvenir towel."

"Truly, the items dreams are made of."

"Hell, I guess I don't know why I liked that trip so much either," he admitted, "though I must remember it more fondly than you. There was something about it I never could forget. I'd never taken a trip like that before. It was different."

"Just the nude beach part, or all of it?" I joked, trying to lighten up the conversation a bit.

"God," he exclaimed. "We were the only ones on that beach under 40. That was not what I planned, or wanted to see for that matter. Where do attractive people go to be naked? Pornos? One couple other than us was at least reasonable, but everyone else was downright scary, like a key party at a rest home."

"And what about that old guy fishing?"

"Man! Casting off into the surf with nothing but a hat! Wasn't he afraid to snag something? Fish hooks have barbs, definitely not something I'd do."

"I don't even like fishing," I remarked, "with or without scrotums, particularly snagged ones."

"Anyway," Thomas said, "that was my favorite vacation."

He went silent after that, lying on the seat. It seemed like there was more going on than that, more behind his question than just wanting to reminisce about a trip to Daytona. But, he stopped talking. Maybe that was it. Maybe I'd been paranoid.

"But there's something that gets me," Thomas said, sitting up. There was more after all. He looked a little agitated.

"What's that?"

"What are we supposed to do with memories like that?"

I looked at him. I wasn't seeing what he was getting at. I mean, it was a vacation. What else did you do with it? You remembered. It wasn't like it had much actual value to us, but that didn't matter. Good memories were good memories as far as I was concerned. I must have visibly showed my confusion, because Thomas tried to explain.

"My favorite vacation, some of my favorite memories, and they're all tied up with you. You're even in all the pictures. If I want to be happy and remember, I can't do it without thinking of you as well."

"So?" I swallowed.

"So? That's the past, Cassandra. I can't think that way about it anymore. Not being with Kate."

"I see."

"But I can't help it," he protested. "I want my happy times; I want to remember that trip. What are we supposed to do with memories like that?" he asked.

"I don't know," I answered. I was definitely being honest.

Dinner

Thomas arranged the sweetener packets in rows according to color. Pink in one pile, blue in another, and white in a third. Then he put them back, sorted appropriately, into the holder that also held the pie menu and the salt and pepper shakers.

I didn't know why he felt the need to do that. We didn't need the packets for anything. Sure, we'd messed them up using them to keep score in Armistice, but there was no need to clean them up. Certainly there was no need to restore them to original condition, like a Boy Scout leaving a campsite. If we never left, no one would care. If we ever got out, the busser would fix it.

Still, I didn't stop him. It occupied him for a while, and watching him work occupied me.

"Thomas," I said after he was done, "what is your position on the pancake dilemma?"

He looked at me. "Cassandra," he replied slowly, "I was not aware there was a pancake dilemma. You're the pancake aficionado, so why don't you enlighten me?"

Of course, he spoke in a facetious tone. Nice, but facetious. Think of kids asking questions on educational programming. He knew I wanted him to ask, and ask he did. It was gratifying to have a helpful conversation participant once in a while.

"Well, surely you agree that pancakes are nature's most perfect food substance."

"Some of the time," he equivocated.

"I mean, when done right. Think fluffy buttermilk pancakes, perfect in texture, temperature, and consistency. Think pancakes lightly buttered and covered, not soaked, in syrup. Preferably the syrup is maple, but pancake syrup may be acceptable in some circumstances. Think three, three is the magical number for pancakes. Are we clear as to the underlying conditions?"

"Yep."

"And is this not, exactly as I've described, nature's most wonderful culinary treat?"

"All right," he agreed. "I'll go with that."

"However," I challenged, "is it not also one of the most fragile of the entire food kingdom?"

His brow furrowed. "How so?"

"There are a million different factors that go into the making of perfect pancakes. When the universe is in complete alignment, angels voice their heavenly choir. However, if a single humor is out of balance, the devil dances upon the Earth. They may still be tasty, but they are only a disappointing shadow of what was expected. It's akin to thinking Alec Baldwin is going to be in a movie only to find out it's Daniel."

"I know they're pretty tasty at first, but if I eat too many then I feel like puking all of a sudden."

I shook my head. "Utterly irrelevant. That's actually an aspect of perfection. Nature has built-in portion control. When you're supposed to stop, they don't taste good anymore. No other food in the wild contains such an advancement."

"All right," he said, "then you give an example."

"I will." I cleared my throat. "Do you cook pancakes at home?"

"Not really," Thomas admitted. "I tend to have them more when I'm out."

"Exactly! Though they are relatively easy to make, using a batter mix or some such abomination, it is better to rely on experts. The end product is far more appealing."

"Agreed."

"But," I paused, "even relying on experts, do you often achieve a perfect pancake experience? Or, is something else more likely? Something much more disheartening and tragic?"

"I feel like I'm being coached."

"I'll ignore that," I said. "No, even at restaurants, perfectly done pancakes, which should be mandated by law, are hard to find. More often than not, the pancakes are too something."

"Such as?"

"Too cold, so as to be tasteless and disgusting. Too cooked, so as to have a vinyl-like shell."

"How about undercooked?" Thomas asked. "You know, when they end up gritty, or having that sour, doughy taste."

"Good example," I congratulated. "Though, sometimes the lack of firm fluffiness, or other textural issues, may actually be the result of an improper batter mix, such as inadequate amounts of real buttermilk, as opposed to cooking time issues. Still, failure to hit the exact right cooking temperature and time, that golden 'sweet' spot, does bear its share of the blame."

"Okay, pancakes are hard to get right. I'm with you."

"Even when the cooking and ingredients are absolutely perfect," I continued, "things can still go wrong. The pancakes can still take too long to get to the table."

Thomas gave me an exaggerated, fake frown. I loved it when he had the humor to play along, even though this was serious.

"The diner may also bear some responsibility. Even when the pancakes arrive in perfect condition, the diner may ignore them in favor of another food, such as bacon, and allow them to get unacceptably cold. Frankly, pancake priority should also be mandated by law. Beyond that, the diner may forget the butter, or butter after allowing the pancakes to cool so that it does not melt. In some cases, the diner may even over-syrup the pancakes, or under-syrup, or even both in some strange situations."

"I get that. I don't do it," Thomas insisted, "but I get what you're saying."

"All right," I concluded, "therefore we can see how truly fragile the beautiful and marvelous wild pancake is. So many different factors have to align; the chances of it working are slim. Yet, sometimes it does all work. When it does, there is nothing it can be compared to. It is truly proof of the existence of God, difficult to obtain as it is."

"Okay," Thomas prompted. "Consider that all taken as given; what's next?"

"What do you mean what's next? That's it; that's the end. The perfect pancake is amazing, but such a thing is extremely difficult to locate. It's the unicorn of foods."

"No, I mean where's the dilemma?"

"Ah. I didn't realize you were ready to move onto that part. You must be more specific."

"Sorry," Thomas laughed.

"Apology accepted," I went on. "The dilemma is whether or not you would choose to pursue the pancake. You will attain ultimate bliss if you find the perfect one, but you may have to suffer a great deal of imperfect pancakes on the journey there. Truly, the search may be quite long and arduous."

Thomas considered. Well . . . he at least pretended to. I'm not sure if he'd caught on enough to take that seriously or not. He looked like he was being serious, but it was hard to tell. I couldn't be sure.

"Well?" I asked.

"It's too bad I can't be guaranteed perfect pancakes every time," he offered. "I'd go for it for sure."

I nodded. "Everyone would. Of course, then there would be no dilemma, so I can't take that as your final position."

"I'm sorry." He shook his head. "I'm not sure I would do it, not keep searching all the time like that."

"You'd go for something easier?" I asked. "Something that led to less peril but also to more certain pleasure?"

"I probably would," he admitted. "Maybe waffles or French toast, maybe even a blintz or two."

"I thought as much," I said. "Not everyone is strong enough to hang on for that kind of ordeal. The pancake demands a heavy price of its devotees. Not everyone can afford to pay, or is prepared to even if they can."

"I'd never give them up entirely," Thomas offered, "They come with a bunch of other stuff I like, like a side. I'd still have them, trying for the good ones, but I would eat the other stuff in the meantime."

"Understood."

"Frankly," he went on, "it's too bad we can't see what's wrong when a set of pancakes comes out and travel back in time to warn the cook. Say the pancakes are overdone. Pop back a few minutes earlier in the kitchen and yell: Dude! Take those off the griddle, they're done!"

"Or the same if they're undercooked," I said. "Just grab the cook in a headlock so he doesn't take them off until they're ready."

"Exactly," he said. "Or sneak back and grab the pancakes yourself if they're going to sit too long. Then I could have good pancakes all the time and not have to put up with the heartache."

"That sounds a bit like Quantum Leap," I said.

"It might," Thomas admitted.

"Traveling through time . . . setting right breakfasts that once went wrong?"

"Okay," he protested. "It is Quantum Leap. I'm sorry I didn't think of something original. There's a lot of pressure here and I'm doing my best."

"I'm not sure it works anyway," I said.

"Why not? Other than the time travel part . . . ."

"Still no dilemma. You wouldn't be risking anything for the pancakes. That's still just wishing they'd come out perfect and saying you'd choose them if they did. The only difference is that time travel is hypothetically involved."

"I see your point," Thomas admitted.

"I do like the idea, though," I agreed. "I'd end up with much more satisfying pancakes that way."

"I know," Thomas said. "There's always this urge to go back in time and fix things. I guess it's just something people want to do."

"Maybe so," I conceded. "At least as far as pancakes are concerned."

Sides

Let's say a pet shop has an employee it's pretty happy with. He does really good work, knows the area well pet-wise, and has a good idea about what pet owners want. The pet shop never has cause to complain about him; he does his work and does it well.

He even has ideas to expand the business. The pet shop might not have the resources to grow the way the employee imagines right now, but they recognize that his ideas are good. Maybe they even tell the employee that. They'll probably work on using his idea in the future when they do have the resources; it just won't happen right now.

However, the employee isn't happy. The pet shop treats him well, but he wants to be part of a growing business, one that is growing right now. Life is too short, after all. He thinks the pet shop won't ever want to take risks. They told him they would when the time was right, but he thinks he'll be waiting forever.

Now, the pet shop doesn't want the employee to be unhappy. They know about the problem; they aren't blind. They talk to the employee about his concerns, show him their financial statements and projections for when things would be more suitable. It's all they can do, really. There is still a business to run, and businesses can only take certain kinds of risks. That's just the way things are.

But, really, this isn't enough for the employee. He needs to be using his ideas, bringing them into the world. They burn inside him. He has to get them out.

It isn't recognition that he craves. He needs to put his ideas into tangible form. He's compelled, a quite admirable thing actually. It feels like such a waste to him that more isn't being done. Things need to be done; it's the way of things.

The pet shop feels bad, but what can they do? It would be irresponsible to put the fulfillment needs of an employee ahead of the rational current needs of their business, no matter how valuable the employee is. Bottom line, they have to do what they think is prudent. They are business people, after all. They're in this to make money and not to risk losing it.

So, the situation goes on. The employee can't be happy and, though they'd like to, the pet shop can't make him happy. All they can do is hope he isn't all that unhappy.

Except, he is. Sooner or later, he starts looking around at other pet shops. It isn't like the pet shop is the only one out there; he has options. Somebody else might be in a position to actually do something with his ideas, even if the pet shop isn't. He's a good employee; somebody might want him.

And, somebody does. A pet emporium starts talking to the employee. They're looking for somebody with ideas to expand. Their situation is right for it in just the kinds of ways the employee thought of, but they don't have anybody with ideas. They can give the employee what he needs, a chance to implement his ideas. He only has to leave the pet shop to go over to the pet emporium.

Mind you, the employee isn't really happy with the situation either. He loves working at the pet shop. He doesn't want to leave. Still, he doesn't feel like he has a choice. He has to act. His need is greater than his love for the pet shop.

Now, don't feel too bad for the pet shop. They know what's going on. They might not know the exact specifics, but they've got the gist. They wish they could do something to stop it, but they know they can't. Instead, they operate their business from day to day, knowing something is going to happen. It's like driving a car with an oil leak when you've got no money to fix it. You can put more oil in once in a while, but that's about all you can do. You know you should wait to drive it until you fix it, but you've got to get to work until then or you'll never have the money. You cringe every time you drive, knowing that at any moment the engine could lock.

And lock the engine did. Sooner or later, the employee gave his notice. The pet shop could have done something then, but they still weren't ready for the expansion. Instead, they had to wait out those two long weeks, thinking the whole time that at the end the employee would be gone.

I really don't need to tell you what happens at this point. The two weeks run out and the employee leaves. On the first day after the expiration of the employee's notice, the pet shop opens and looks around at the fact that the employee isn't there.

Frankly, the pet shop misses the employee. They really liked him and his work. Business has to go on, but they couldn't imagine who could replace him. Every day, they can't ignore the employee's absence. They don't even really know where he went. However, they do still go on. The business even prospers, though the pet shop can't help but feel they'd do even better if the employee was still around.

Eventually, the pet shop learns that the employee now works at the pet emporium. After all, it isn't like the pet shop doesn't stay current on its competitors, and the pet business is open to the public, so it makes sense that they would learn at some point. The employee certainly didn't try to hide anything. He just never specifically mentioned where he was going. The pet shop never asked.

Of course, the pet emporium is expanding based on the employee's ideas. That was the whole point of the employee going over. Remember? The pet emporium is doing great; the employee's ideas are working well.

Maybe that's one reason the pet shop learns about where the employee is working so quickly. Sure, they would have figured it out eventually. However, one of their competitors is suddenly growing exponentially, using some very familiar sounding ideas . . . . Well, that's pretty noticeable.

Still, it's not like they can do much about it. They know where the employee works. They know he's expanding the pet emporium using ideas he'd offered to them. What of it? They had their chance. The time hadn't been right and that was that.

After all, the pet shop never owned the employee. They might have wanted to, but that wasn't possible so there was no use in entertaining that notion. That was against the law, unfortunately.

Frankly, the pet shop hadn't even spoken to the employee since he worked his last day. He never stopped by, never called or anything. The pet shop never heard so much as a hello. They even still had some of the personal items he'd decorated his work area with, but hadn't come to get. The pet shop wasn't sure he ever would.

What was the pet shop supposed to do? The employment relationship with the employee was over. Finished. Caput. Stone dead. They might have missed him, but what's over is over. Right?

But then, the pet shop ran into the employee at a big pet product convention. They didn't avoid each other or anything. Sure, they hadn't talked since the employee left, but it wasn't like they were enemies. There was no reason they couldn't be civil. After all, their employment relationship had gone on for a long time. They had history. There was no ignoring that.

And it was cool, getting a chance to catch up like that. The pet shop was actually glad to hear the employee was doing so well. They certainly didn't begrudge him his success. In fact, they felt he deserved it.

What they weren't prepared for, however, was the employee's comment about missing his days at the pet shop. It really threw them for a loop. They weren't sure what the employee meant by that, or how they were supposed to take it. They weren't even sure how they felt about it, regardless of the employee's intentions. In short, they were confused.

Regardless of what it meant and how it felt, the comment had been made. There was no getting around that. Sooner or later, the pet shop was going to have to figure out how they wanted to respond.

I mean, were they supposed to ask him to come back? Their situation had changed dramatically. They were now in a position to use the employee's suggestions, and they wanted to. Since the situation was finally different they wanted to expand, and expand just like the employee had imagined. They wished they still had him more than ever.

But, was he willing to come back? Was that what he wanted?

Did he miss the pet shop that much?

After all, what was there to draw him back? The pet emporium let him implement all his ideas already. The pet shop could do that, too, but they had nothing more to offer. No additional incentives, and they'd said no for so long. Would he even believe them? Or, would he think they were just trying to destroy the pet emporium? Or, even him? Just for revenge?

Even if he believed them and wanted to come back, did he want to enough to leave where he was? He was established there. He was wrapped up in the implementation of his plans. Could he tear himself away mid-go?

The pet shop wasn't sure. They didn't handle uncertainty well. If things weren't clear then they didn't act. They were cautious. But, maybe they had to act this time. Maybe the employee would come back and regret it.

Did they want all that? Was that what they really, really wanted? They didn't know.

Meanwhile, every second they didn't act, the pet shop felt the situation change. The employee's ties to his new job got stronger. The pet emporium implemented more of the employee's ideas and grew more prosperous. Things kept changing, getting more and more complicated.

Still, why did they wait? The worst thing the employee could do was say no, that they had misunderstood what he had meant. That wasn't so bad, was it?

Of course, I might be talking about something other than a pet shop here.

Beverages

There was actually a manager at the Village Inn. I don't know why that would possibly come as a surprise, since all Village Inns have managers, but I hadn't talked about her before so I thought it merited saying.

We'd only seen her once. She was on the way to her little manager office. I peeked in the door a little, but she slammed it shut it pretty fast. That was all we saw of her, which is saying something given how long we'd been there. No walking around asking customers how their visit was, no keeping tabs on how the employees were doing their jobs, none of that.

I don't know, maybe she had a lot of bookkeeping to do. Maybe she was trying to work out some 'Grand Central Station' difficulty level scheduling issue. Whatever she was doing, she was always in that little room.

Mind you, it wasn't like the restaurant was falling apart. Everything seemed to run smooth. The Village Inn received ingredients, paid invoices, scheduled workers and paid them, received food orders, served food which customers ate, and did everything else that was supposed be done at a Village Inn. Maybe things ran on their own, an automated child of a perfectly designed system, or maybe the manager had some sneaky way of taking care of everything without leaving her office.

Of course, I didn't know for sure that all those things got done; I assumed. I told you I'd never been in the kitchen, but the front house didn't look like it had any problems. One would think that any issue would have shown up fast, like them not having pancakes or something. Either way, I gave the manager credit, however she ran things.

I got a pretty clear picture of her the one time we did see her. She was over six feet tall, towering over me at least, and was too heavy even for that height. Her hair looked like a marine flattop gone long in the back, kind of mullet-ish, and she dressed like a Marine's idea of business casual.

I'm serious, though I intend no disrespect to her or Marines. After all, Marines don't exactly spend their time in business meetings. Village Inn managers I've seen tend to dress that way, or fast food managers who somehow think being a manager means they're executives even though they work fast food. Rough-wear slacks with a short-sleeved white button-up shirt. Plus a narrow black tie that had better be a clip-on since it looks like one anyway. That's the restaurant manager's code, along with no overtime.

The manager at that Village Inn didn't deviate, though she did strain the buttons of the short-sleeved white shirt a bit. She may have been a bit fat, but she did seem to have her share of muscle in there. Imagine a female linebacker at church.

I couldn't blame her for hiding out. I would have too if I looked like that, and if I had a key to the office. Still, she was clearly the manager. You certainly had to give her that much.

Hiding in her office like she did, it was almost impossible not to make up something about her. I mean, she was right there . . . but she wasn't. I was curious, and when I get curious I start making things up. That's just something about me. My brain has to fill in the holes.

I should explain; the manager's office was right off the dining room. Obviously, this proved her status since she was neither back in the kitchen nor sitting in the dining room. There was a door on the wall, near the bathrooms, that locked. I could tell that much; she used a key tied to her wrist with one of those stretchy plastic coil bands the time I saw her go in.

I didn't see much in that brief moment, but I saw enough. It was little more than a broom closet with a desk, stacks of paper everywhere. I was sure I saw a motivational poster as well, something about an eagle and a mouse. That was more than enough to get my mind started. I mean, it was bad enough to be stuck in the booth. Being stuck in that little cubicle-office would have been far worse.

But not for the manager. For her, it was the best possible place she could be in the Village Inn. That's why she stayed in there all the time. Not because she had to, but by choice.

Maybe she played music in there all day, or fought solitaire on the computer. She might have even done some work once in a while, whatever she could do while she was back there. Nobody could bother her unless she let them in, unless they called on the phone of course, because that door automatically locked when it shut. She was in her own tiny little world, and that was good enough for her. It was good because she was doing her job, but she was away from the Village Inn.

You see, the manager had a terrible fear of Village Inns. It was paralyzing, all-encompassing. There was nothing she dreaded more than a Village Inn. Snakes? Death? REO Speedwagon? Nope, for her it was Village Inns.

Now, it might seem silly for her to be a manager of a Village Inn if she was afraid of them. However, it all made sense when you knew the story. Or, of course, when you made one up.

How would it make sense? What kind of story would explain it? Well, the manager wasn't always afraid of Village Inns, not all her life certainly. Once you know that then everything falls into place.

In fact, when she was a small child, she adored Village Inns. They were the happiest places on Earth for her. Disneyland? Six Flags? No thanks; she would not have been interested. She would have taken a trip to Village Inn over any of that. France? South America? She wouldn't have gone, not unless you told her they had Village Inns. She had a one-track mind as far as Village Inns were concerned, and in her mind Village Inns were almost always concerned.

You see, her Grammy used to take her to Village Inn. As long as she could remember, Saturday mornings meant Village Inn. That was what her and her Grammy did together, their time. And, of course, she certainly loved her Grammy.

She used to get the same thing every time: pancakes. Of course, they weren't ordinary pancakes. That wouldn't have done at all. They had to have fried eggs for eyes, no runny yolks please, and two strips of crispy bacon for a smiley mouth. There was even a nose, a big ball of spray whipped cream with a cherry in the center. The manager, as a child of course, thought it looked like a bald clown.

For the longest time, it was just what her Grammy ordered for her, back when she was too little to decide on her own. It was much better than what her parents would order for her at Perkins, those gross potato pancakes, so of course she liked Grammy better. Obviously, she liked Village Inn better, too.

When she got bigger, her Grammy tried to get her to try other things. Things like waffles, or skillets, or even omelets, but the manager only wanted her kid's pancakes. Nothing else was good enough, wouldn't even come close. She insisted. Then her Grammy would always laugh and order the kid's pancakes like the manager wanted.

That was what her Grammy called those pancakes, by the way. The manager never knew if that was their real name or if her Grammy made it up and ordered them that way. When she was little, she couldn't read so she didn't know if they were on the menu that way or not. When she was older, she couldn't even bring herself to touch the menu to be able to check.

Now, her Grammy wasn't a bad Grammy, not just because she let the manager have pancakes with whipped cream every Saturday. It may not have been the most nutritious breakfast, but her Grammy did love her very much. Her Grammy knew the manager's parents made her eat only healthy stuff the rest of the week, so pancakes once in a while wouldn't hurt anything, and the manager's parents never knew because they weren't invited on Saturdays.

No, the pancakes were a very special treat for a very special little girl. That's what her Grammy always told her, and her Grammy wouldn't have lied. That's why she loved her Grammy, and that's why she loved Village Inn.

But, there had to be a but or we'd never get to why she was afraid later, one Saturday her Grammy had a heart attack while they were eating breakfast. Their food had arrived and the manager was eating the whipped cream nose, her Grammy taking a bite of sausage, when her Grammy made a noise.

The manager, of course, didn't know what a heart attack was at the time, she only learned that later. When she looked up from her pancakes she just knew that her Grammy was all red in the face. She breathed funny. Holding her arm and twisting up her face, her Grammy tried to say something, but she only sputtered. Then she fell on the floor. The manager didn't know what was wrong.

Now, the manager's Grammy didn't die. Even I wouldn't imagine something like that to her. Luckily, the other people at the Village Inn came rushing over to help. They took her Grammy away in a big white ambulance van.

The hospital made her Grammy better, but she never got all the way better. She stayed pretty sick after that. The manager's parents said they had to put Grammy in a home so she could get help when she needed it. Either way, Grammy didn't go out on her own after that, and there were no more Saturdays at Village Inn.

In fact, no one took the manager to Village Inn ever again. Like I said before, her parents liked Perkins. The manager didn't ask anymore, not without Grammy. Village Inns were cut off from the manager at that point, like they didn't exist. They were places she couldn't go. It wasn't that she didn't love them anymore, just that they were no longer for her.

At some point the manager started to feel uneasy whenever she walked near a Village Inn. Soon, she felt a chill whenever she saw one. Even the mention of the name made her a little bit sad.

As she got older, it only got worse. Sometimes she would lay awake at night, her pulse racing and her body drenched in sweat, unable to not think of Village Inns. She did anything she could to think of something else and fall asleep, but Village Inns dominated her unwilling mind.

She had nightmares, strange nightmares. Nothing would happen. She wasn't even inside the Village Inns in the nightmares.

Her Grammy wasn't either, nobody was. Instead, there was always a Village Inn by itself, eerily empty. That's all the dream was, a still frame of an ominous Village Inn, bare, promising the most terrible things. The manager always awoke screaming.

It baffled her. Even after her Grammy got sick, she still loved Village Inns. She certainly wasn't afraid of them then. Where had the fear come from? Why had it come?

The manager had no idea. She never would, in fact. All she ever knew was the dread, the dread that the Village Inn was out there waiting for her. She could not escape it, not while there was even the idea of Village Inns in the world.

Even beyond the terror itself, the very fact of the dread made her sad. Village Inns had been the best part of the world for her, but suddenly they were the worst. She never felt the happiness she had once known on those Saturday mornings. It seemed to be gone from life, gone with her love for Village Inn.

She felt that somehow the only way to reclaim that happiness was through Village Inn. If only she could make the dread go away, then she thought she could go into Village Inns again and be happy. Somehow, she thought, it would all be like before.

But, how could she do it? How could the manager fight a fear she didn't understand? She didn't have money for therapists, and she didn't believe they could help anyway. Certainly, she couldn't imagine explaining to one that she feared Village Inn but she had to be able to go in them or her life would be over. No, she was on her own.

She heard things about aversion therapy, facing fears. The idea completely terrified her, but she didn't have any choice. What could she do? She got a job as a manager of a Village Inn.

It was the first time in years she could remember feeling elated. Finally, things were going to be different. Finally, she would be at peace. She had taken control; she was going to take her life back.

Unfortunately, it didn't work. Every day, she ran to the little office as fast as she could. The fear would only escalate until she did. When she was away from work, all she could think of was how she had to go back the next day. Even in the little room, with the door locked to keep the Village Inn at bay, she could feel it hulking down around her, waiting for her to come out.

Maybe that's why facing her fear never worked. After all, she never really faced it. She went into the Village Inn, but she was almost always in the office. Whenever she wasn't, she was thinking about going there. Really, she spent almost no time in the Village Inn itself. Instead of confronting the Village Inn, she was focusing her life on fearing it.

She had created her own prison. Every day she had to be as close as possible to the thing she feared most, all from the hope that it would someday lead to great joy. All she could do was to go into work each day, each time hoping things would finally be different.

That's why she was in her office all the time, because she was waiting for change. I felt bad for her, since because of us she would have to wait in there forever. I would have changed everything for her if I could have . . . but of course, I couldn't.

THURSDAY

Breakfast

It was finally a problem that Kate was in the bathroom, because I had to go. I found that strange, the fact that I had to go. After all, despite all the coffee I'd been drinking, I almost never had to go to the bathroom while we were at the Village Inn. However, I certainly had to go at that moment. Bad.

Mind you, having to go to the bathroom at the same time Kate was in there normally wouldn't have been a problem. There were two stalls; it wasn't a single person bathroom. Technically I could go, unless someone was using the other stall. Besides, it wasn't as if Kate and I had never gone to the bathroom in a pair before back when we were still friends. Women go to the bathroom in pairs, right?

Still, I wasn't sure I wanted to be alone with her right then. Not as alone as a bathroom could be, and certainly not that alone with the sort of thoughts I was thinking after talking to Thomas. I could only see disaster level possibilities.

I always had this odd fear that other people were mind readers and not telling me. When thinking things I wouldn't want nearby people to know, the fear only doubled. I'd start seeing everything as signs they knew my thoughts and my head would go nuts trying to think fake thoughts to cloud the psychic airwaves. It made social interaction a bit awkward.

Kate was almost worse than other people, even when we were friends. She had a habit of finishing my sentences, or of knowing the perfect gift to give me. She even, on more than one occasion, randomly bought accessories for a surprise gift I was about to give her. It was probably that she knew me really well because we hung out all the time, but it fed my psychic paranoia like nothing else. Of course, maybe that's the reason she did it. She always did like messing with people.

But it wasn't like I had a choice. I needed the bathroom. So, I got up from the booth and wandered on in.

I didn't see her at first. I thought maybe she had vanished. I didn't see anybody; the bathroom looked empty. Of course, she was in one of the stalls with the door closed, like any other sane person using the bathroom. At least she never saw my confusion. She would have gotten a chuckle out of that.

Kate had taken the smaller stall, the one across the sink from the bathroom door. I walked quickly past her locked stall door to the open one and went inside. She'd unintentionally, I hoped, left me the handicap stall. I locked my door in case she came out, or in case anyone else came in. Obviously. Everybody locks those stall doors.

The handicap stall wasn't bad. It was roomy, even if I had no need for the railings and such. It was clean, too. I always felt bad when people messed up handicap stalls, but this one wasn't particularly frightening. However, the additional room made me feel like I was even more alone with Kate.

I quickly went to the bathroom. She hadn't said anything yet and I was hoping she hadn't figured out it was me. Then I could get done, hurry up and wash, and get out of there before she came out of her stall.

"Does yours have any graffiti?" Kate asked.

Crap. "No," I replied, "it's clean."

She sighed. "Mine too. How disappointing."

I waited for her to keep talking. I wasn't sure if I was supposed to say something or not. She could have been going anywhere with that.

"At least I'd have something to read," she eventually continued. "Something interesting."

"Or lewd at least."

It did seem odd that there wasn't any kind of writing on the walls. People always wrote things. Men's rooms, women's rooms, it was all the same. The content only differed a little, perhaps some on the amount, but nowhere near as much as you might think. I guessed the Village Inn cleaned it up too fast. It was a family place, after all.

"You know," she said, "I always wanted to go on a road trip and write dirty limericks on bathroom walls wherever I stopped. I don't know why, but it seemed like such a fun thing to do. Maybe I've got a hidden vandal streak in me."

"Maybe."

"It's this unique kind of communication, subversive but connective at the same time. Late night people in hidden places shouting silently to each other that they are out there, that they are alive. People saying things to each other, or trying to at least."

"Seems to be mostly dirty things," I commented.

"Well sure, their notes say they are alive and they think crude things. It doesn't make them any less alive, just like the fact that they never see each other doesn't make them any less connected. It's the only thing they can think of to talk about."

I went quiet again. I had already finished and pulled up my sweats, but I still sat there. It felt awkward to leave before she finished talking.

"I got to do a road trip like that once," she admitted.

"Yeah?"

"It was back in high school. Debate. The teacher got a bus and took the whole team to DC so we could listen to a Congressional session. I guess it was supposed to show us real debate or something. It was kind of stupid."

"Did you write limericks when you stopped?"

"I hated all the other kids," she confided. "The limerick thing was the only reason I went. Otherwise, I was going to tell the teacher I had strep throat and had to stay home. He wouldn't dare risk the throats of his star debaters, which I wasn't one of, by the way."

"Well, at least you got to do your limericks, right? You got to live at least one dream."

"That's just it," she yelled, or at least seemed to with the way it echoed in the small bathroom. I worried someone outside would hear us, think some nasty thing was going on in the bathroom, but the dining room was probably too loud for that. "I finally got out there on a road trip, and I'd forgot the most important part!"

"A pen?"

"No, I didn't know any limericks! I had nothing to write; I couldn't think of a single thing."

"How is that possible?" I asked. "Everybody knows at least one dirty limerick. They're everywhere."

"One," she demanded. "Say one right now."

And like that, my mind went blank. Every limerick I'd ever heard, it was like they'd never existed. You'd think with as often as I'd heard them that I'd remember one, but I didn't.

"I . . . can't," I finally admitted.

"See? You think you know some, everybody does, but you don't. You don't really listen when anyone tells one, so you never remember it later. You just groan and then the memory dies."

"Guess so."

"I thought for sure I knew dozens, hundreds. My uncles used to tell them whenever they got drunk. Still, out there finally ready to do it, I had nothing."

Even I felt a little bad for Kate then, sitting together in a Village Inn crapper. "So you didn't write any?"

"God," she sighed. "I couldn't do that. I just couldn't. There was only one kid on the bus who knew one, and I had to give him a hand job so he'd tell me. Then I wrote that same damn limerick on every bathroom wall I came across on that trip."

"Wow."

"Yeah, and it wasn't even a good one. It went: There once was a man from Vernass, who had two balls made out of brass. In stormy weather, he'd click them together, and sparks would shoot out of his ass."

I thought about the limerick for a minute. "It isn't really that dirty," I commented. "I mean, it says 'balls' and 'ass,' but that's about it."

"I know," she groaned, "and the kid smelled like bad plain yogurt. It was horrible."

I looked up at the bare stall walls around me. "It's too bad we don't have a pen," I said. "After having gone through that, you should write it here, too."

Lunch

We came out of the bathroom and headed back to the booth. Something about the conversation had made me not want to cut out like I'd planned, even though it didn't feel like it'd quite gone as she'd expected. I don't know what she'd been thinking, but somehow there seemed like something more was supposed to happen. I guessed I kind of felt for her and hung out a bit with her in the bathroom.

I thought we were done, though, so when we got back in the dining room I just went to sit down again. Right as I was about to, Kate grabbed my elbow and started pulling me to the front of the restaurant. She was smiling so I wasn't worried or anything.

"Hey!" Thomas said, holding up his hands. "What the hell?"

She waved him off, dismissing him. "We'll be back," she told him. "Just keep yourself busy a bit longer."

I nodded and went along with it. I felt like humoring Kate. Besides, I'd sat with Thomas a lot longer than I'd been in the bathroom. Kate and I could hang a little while longer. It'd be a change if nothing else.

Kate steered us up front by the doors, right past the pie case. I thought she was going to try to take us outside at first, futile as that would have been to try those doors again, but we sat on the long bench in the entryway instead. Kate sat right next to me and put one leg over the other, pretty impressive considering how tight her skinny jeans were. She put her hands on her knee and kicked one foot. The bobbing motion caused her blond ponytail to twitch like the tail of a pouncing housecat.

We sat there for a couple of minutes, not doing anything. I didn't see why Kate had pulled us over there. She was looking around the restaurant. I was looking at Kate.

"Okay," I said finally, "what are we doing?"

"Can't you guess?"

"Apparently not," I replied.

"It's been a while," she conceded. "I'll give you a hand then. Social graces inquisition."

Then it clicked. It really should have before; we used to play it all the time, back before our falling out. It wasn't the nicest game, but sometimes being catty and picking other people apart made me feel better. Identify, classify, and sentence. No appeals.

Of course, it really wasn't that mean. As long as you didn't actually say any of the things to the accused, then what was the harm? That was one of the core rules anyway, not actually letting the accused hear. Judgment was supposed to be final, removed, and creative.

"I'll go first," she said, scanning the restaurant.

I looked around as well. Who would she focus on first? This was a Village Inn; there were plenty of choices, all depending on your personal taste. You couldn't go wrong.

"There," she said, nodding at a couple halfway across the restaurant.

I examined them. The man and woman didn't strike me as interesting, but they had a squalling baby in a high chair next to their table. He was a plump little bald boy in a white onesie with multi-colored stains on it. At least, I think he was a boy; I've never been able to tell. Flailing his arms, he was bawling loud enough that his face had gone red like a lobster. Clearly, that sort of food resemblance was out of place at a Village Inn.

The couple didn't even seem to notice. They were chatting happily and eating, like perhaps their waitress had inexplicably dropped off a baby and never said why. Not knowing what to do since they didn't have any kids of their own, they continued their meal and ignored the little bundle of 'joy.' He didn't even have any food, not even any Cheerios to keep him busy. The couple didn't even look at him the whole time I was staring.

Now, I know people with kids have it tough. No matter how good a job they do, someone will always be judging them. Harshly. Worse, later on their own kid will tell them what a horrible job they did. Real gratitude. People do the best they can, though some people really do need to do better, and the last thing they need is one more childless person putting in his or her own expert opinion.

Sure, it looked bad. But . . . I didn't know the real story there. Maybe the baby had been fed already and just liked screaming. The parents had to eat, too. Besides, maybe there was nothing they could do for him. Maybe he needed to yell himself out. What did I know? You'd think they'd know better than me.

Of course, it was also possible they were neglectful monsters. In the end, that's what I had to assume. After all, empathy was not part of that particular game.

"Broken condom," I said.

"Ooh," Kate replied. "Good one."

"They were never intended to reproduce," I continued, "but due to massive prophylactic failure, the universe was forced to let them become parents. Luckily for the child, they're not the most organized people, or they might have done something."

"And the sentence?"

I paused, considering them. If they did something for the baby, then maybe I'd be merciful. Or not. I waited for the whim to strike me, also part of the rules. There were a lot of rules for social graces inquisition.

"They've already been sentenced," I replied. "This is it."

She looked over at them. "Apt, but we'll need something more. Sentences must be imposed after the offense, not result from it."

"All right," I said. "Then I sentence them to desire children the day after the baby grows up, moves out, and wants nothing to do with them. Suitable?"

"Very Cat's in the Cradle," she said. "I like it."

"Thanks. My pick now?"

"Indeed." She smiled.

I'd already selected, holding my choice in reserve to seem more confident, which was another rule. I motioned at a girl in a belly-baring shirt.

"Eww," Kate said.

"Exactly."

I've never been one to jump on people for body imperfections, but there are certain choices that must be made. For example, if your belly rolls down over the waistline of your pants, like that particular girl's, then you probably shouldn't bare it. Just saying.

That girl wasn't even really that heavy, but she had no reason to be sporting a belly-barer. Unless, that is, unless the belly in question refused to be chained by a mere shirt. Regardless, her poor choice did her no justice, and made her subject to our irrelevant authority.

"Easy," Kate said. "She's never mastered spatial relationships. She is literally unaware that certain objects do not fit within the confines of certain other objects."

"Is that an offense?"

"Clearly," she responded. "I'm offended."

"Then what's the sentence?"

Kate paused, pursing her lips. "One hundred years doing nothing but trying to put various shaped blocks into different shaped holes. Early parole is possible if she begins to grasp spatial concepts."

"Interesting," I said. "I'm not used to you showing mercy in this game."

She shrugged. "It's been a while. Anyway, your next one is pit stains over there."

The man in question was a younger guy, could have been 19, eating with a younger girl. He had on a white wife-beater and a bunch of die-cast gold-ish necklaces. Most unfortunately, there were dark yellow half-moons under his arms. Other than that, the wife-beater looked clean.

"Meth?"

"Probably," she muttered. "Doesn't matter. Go."

I couldn't use meth. No, really, I mean I couldn't use meth as his offense. The rules, when we followed that particular part, said we couldn't use the complete literal truth, not if it was easily observed. We were required to expend more effort than that.

"Obviously," I said, "he has uncontrollable guilt over the fact that he is only with that girl for her father's money. Worse, it isn't very much money. It's just a trailer and a beat-up pickup truck. There are even rust holes."

"In which?"

"Both," I replied. "Maybe the girl, too. He feels guilty all the time about it, but can't make himself give up either the truck or the trailer. As a result, he sweats uncontrollably. Strange, chemical-based sweats that stain clothes yellow."

"So why does he wear shitty tank tops? Something else would be less noticeable."

"So he can change them as often as possible and throw the old ones away," I said. "White wife-beaters are the only thing cheap enough to be disposable. Anyway, he'd stain black just as bad. He buys those shirts six to a pack and goes through as many in a single day. Heck, he just put that one on in the restroom before they ordered. Look at it already."

Kate snickered.

"I sentence him to 30 hours washing jock straps for the entire starting line of the Chicago Bears," I went on. "Plus, he has to give up the truck, though he can keep the trailer. Of course, that presumes he ever gets them from the girl's father."

"Of course," Kate agreed. "Give me another one. Something challenging this time."

I thought about it, scanning the room to see if anyone more interesting had shown himself or herself. I gestured to a tiny, ancient woman all the way back in the corner.

Kate squinted to see better. "Is she pouring sugar packets over a slice of pecan pie? Tell me I'm not seeing that right. Nobody would do that. With that gooey filling already? Nobody."

"She is," I confirmed. "At least six or seven packets already. Although, I think that last one was actually Sweet'N Low."

"This one's going to take some doing," Kate said. "If nothing else, to get over the fact that she's doing that enough to be able to think of something. Look! She's doing another!"

"I think that one was NutraSweet."

"What the hell does she think she's doing?"

"Hey," I reminded Kate, "you wanted someone a little tougher this time."

"Okay, okay," Kate conceded. "Let's see. Greed."

"Obvious."

"No, not like you're thinking," Kate protested. "She's like Scrooge McDuck. Only, she's never had any money. It's terrible on the soul if a person is avaricious and can't get any cash. The greed twisted inside of her, warping her very being, looking for any outlet. Finally, it sprang out as gluttony, though she isn't a glutton. Strange, unusual gluttony."

"Okay," I admitted, "that's a little better."

"But it never satisfies her," Kate went on. "She won't ever feel any pleasure from that sugar-bomb, and whatnot else, she has there. She's driven to do it because of her need to hoard money, but it won't help a single bit. Not even for a microsecond. In the end, sugar isn't money. Gluttony is not avarice."

"Sounds like another case where the crime is going to be the sentence," I remarked. "It sounds pretty punishing by itself."

"Oh no," Kate countered. "I have no sympathy for people who lack the necessary follow-through to indulge their own vices. She can either figure out how to get some money or suffer the additional imposed consequences. Her choice."

"And those are?"

Kate smiled. "Diabetes."

"That's a bit cold," I muttered.

Kate shrugged. "She's not happy anyway. Maybe then she won't be such a freak."

"Presuming she lives that long." I watched the woman finally take a bite. Sugar, and possibly other powders, spilled off the pie all over the tabletop.

"You're next one is right by her," Kate said.

I looked over and there was a middle-aged man sitting a table away from sugar pie. He looked normal, a little gangly perhaps. He had on a nice emerald Oxford shirt and stylish black slacks, probably a CPA or some such thing. Nothing unusual.

Unless, of course, you counted the giant gold women's hoop earrings he had in both ears. I'm talking bracelet-size with little flairs and twists all over. They didn't even look like they went with his head, as if someone had stuck them on him while he slept and he hadn't noticed yet.

I couldn't imagine why he could possibly have them on. They smacked his neck when he turned his head so he had to know, but it didn't make sense. I mean, it would be fine if he was a cross-dresser, but who gender-bends with just ears? Why not glam it up a bit more? It didn't look respectable by just doing the earrings so he might as well go all the way.

And it's not like there was any way he thought these were men's earrings. There just wasn't any way. He knew he was wearing women's earrings with a manly-man professional outfit and haircut, but he didn't care. I couldn't imagine what that reason could be.

"Okay," I said, gearing myself up, "he's actually a professional injury plaintiff. He wears those so people can't stop themselves from making some kind of comment that he can pretend to take offense to. He escalates the incidents into a fight and then makes sure he gets hit first. After that, it's off to his lawyer's office to get filing papers ready for the road to moneytown."

"Interesting," she said. "A leech that makes people latch themselves on."

"Yes, and for his crimes he must repay what he has taken from society. He has to visit senior citizen centers around the country and give seminars on the blood-spatter evidence from the OJ Simpson murder trial. He doesn't get to stop until they all understand, no confusion."

Kate laughed while shaking her head. "I can't believe we stopped doing this," she said.

Dinner

Thomas was playing poker with himself when Kate and I got back. One hand was on his side of the table and another on mine. Apparently, he'd set down one and then pick up the other to play. I didn't know who was winning, but I was sure he'd been bluffing.

Kate dropped into the seat on her side and I slipped into mine. Thomas gathered up the cards and snuck them away. "Have a good time?" he asked.

"The best," Kate replied. "Did you win anything?"

"Sure, but I lost just as much," he laughed.

And like that, we ran out of anything to say. I went back to my now completely cold coffee. Thomas looked out the window. Kate grabbed the pie menu and started reading it. Clearly, we were already bored again. It certainly didn't take long to happen.

The boredom got to me pretty quick. The thoughts in my head got louder the less that was said, and that wasn't a good situation. There were a few things I didn't want to think about right then, and that was about all I could think about. Loud, mentally of course, and repeatedly. I needed to do something to make my head go quiet.

"Let's play shipwreck," I said, grabbing the pie menu holder. I took the sweetener packets out and tossed them to the side. Then I took the salt and pepper shakers out and set them in front of Kate and Thomas, or Thomas and Kate. I'm not sure which way I prefer it.

"I'll play," Thomas agreed, "but I don't know what it is."

"Same here," Kate said, leaning in.

"Simple." I held up the pie menu holder. "This is the boat. One of you is salt and the other is pepper, and you've both been shipwrecked. I'm passing by and you have to convince me to take you on board." I set the pie menu holder in the center of the table.

"Which one of us is which?" Kate asked.

"You guys pick." I smiled.

Kate immediately grabbed the pepper. Thomas, not quick enough, was left with the salt. He reluctantly picked it up. He seemed unsure he wanted it, maybe because he hadn't made any kind of decision in its favor.

"Set them in front of you on the table."

They each did. Kate blocked hers with one hand, as if keeping Thomas away. She even took a napkin and cleaned the pepper scum off the top. Thomas moved his about a little each way by tapping it with his finger.

I sat back and waited. They both looked at me as if they were waiting for me to begin. I wasn't going to make it that easy, though. In this game, I was the one with the boat.

"So . . . how do we play?" Thomas finally asked.

Kate nodded at me in agreement.

"You guys are going to drown at this rate," I said. "The boat is here . . . convince me to pick you up."

"Pick me up," Thomas called to the makeshift boat.

I pushed it closer to him.

"No! Me! Me," Kate said next.

I turned the pie menu holder around and pushed it closer to Kate. "You'll have to be more convincing," I said. "The boat is having trouble making a decision."

Kate's eyes lit up. "Pick me, not him," she said. "You need pepper. Salt is useless."

"Hey!"

"It's true," she told him. "We're shipwrecked and need someone to pick us up, right? Well, that probably means we're on salt water. Not many people get shipwrecked on lakes."

"So?"

"So, she can just pull up some water and let it evaporate. Boom . . . she'd have all the salt she needed. She's already got all she could possibly want, but she's got no easy way to get pepper."

I edged the pie menu holder a bit closer to the pepper shaker. Kate smirked at Thomas. I hoped he'd put up some kind of a fight. Otherwise, the game wouldn't go on for long.

"But that kind of salt isn't clean," he finally exclaimed. "It'd have ocean crap all in it. Besides, it'd take forever to make. I'm clean and ready. No muss, no fuss."

I turned and moved the 'boat' a little closer to the salt shaker, but not much. I didn't want to reward him too far. After all, his argument was pretty weak. In any event, Kate's was better so far.

"The pepper is trying to trick you," he called to the pie menu holder. "Obviously, she can't be trusted. She has an inherently spicy, volatile nature. You shouldn't risk taking her on board. I'm peaceful, though. Salt is familiar."

I edged the pie menu holder closer to his shaker. It was starting to get more interesting. I wondered what direction they would take this, how far they would go.

"But salt is boring! Pepper is interesting. It spices up bland food. You've been at sea . . . you know you crave some flavor. Salt is just more of the same."

The 'boat' switched course, heading for the pepper shaker. I could have done that all day, certainly as long as they could keep it up, selling each other out.

"Pepper makes you sneeze. It'll turn on you if you don't watch out."

"Oh yeah? Salt raises your blood pressure and causes hypertension. He'll kill you."

"At least salt won't kill you on purpose."

"At least with pepper you can see how much you put on," Kate countered. "You can't tell with salt. It hides, because it's sneaky. How many times have you put salt on something and tasted it only to find that it's too much? That never happens with pepper. With pepper, you know. Everything's above board."

"Well, pepper is only a condiment," Thomas shot back. "Salt has other uses. You can de-ice your decks with it. You can use it to make water boil faster."

They had each grabbed their respective shaker and were motioning it toward each other as they shot verbal volleys back and forth. It was almost as if they were making the shakers talk, like the shakers were little faceless puppets. It was pretty heated for a game.

The poor little pie menu holder ship was practically spinning in circles from switching directions so often. Surely, everyone on board would have been seasick, presuming the whole thing hadn't already gotten sucked down into a whirlpool of the ship's own creation. I wasn't a good captain, apparently. I'm sure my imaginary crew wished I were more decisive.

"Pepper has other uses! You can throw it in somebody's face to stop them from attacking," Kate protested.

"You could do the same with salt," Thomas countered. "They just wouldn't sneeze as much."

Honestly, I was kind of enjoying how much they'd gotten into the game. I hadn't expected such fervor, but it was certainly entertaining. I'm not sure why it was fun to pit them against each other like that, but I made no move to stop it.

"Well, he's an asshole," Kate shot back.

"She's got you pretty good there, Thomas. Better think of something quick," I said, acting like I was stirring them up more. I think I was actually trying to diffuse the situation, though.

That's what actually happened, anyway. Thomas opened his mouth, but nothing came out. "Aww," he finally said, "I'm out. I've got nothing."

Kate smirked again. I started pushing the pie menu holder over toward her. I figured I might as well finish the premise of the game.

"Wait a second," Thomas said, "that thing is built to hold both shakers. Why can't you pick me up after you get her?"

I stopped the 'boat.' Then I folded my arms over my chest, sat up straight, and smiled. "Now there's an idea," I said.

"I thought the whole point was fighting which of us you would rescue," Kate argued. "What's the game about if you could have just picked us both up?"

I gave her a smirk of my own. "I never said rescue was an either/or thing. I said you had to convince me to rescue you. He's right, there's room for you both."

I held up the pie menu holder and pointed at the two shaker

spots. "Of course, after you guys fought like that, would you want to be rescued by the same boat?"

Sides

Okay, let's see if we can get all this straight. Maybe it'll all be a little clearer that way.

Originally, I was friends with Kate and more than friends with Thomas. Put the other way, I was originally more than friends with Thomas and friends with Kate. I kept switching it around and I wasn't sure which way I liked better.

Of course, that wasn't originally originally. Originally originally I hadn't met either of them and hadn't even been born. Still, I thought that was a little further back than I really needed to think. There would be too much to consider if I didn't draw some kind of border around things. Way too much to deal with, too many things to ponder.

So, I decided to call 'original' when I was friends with Kate and more than friends with Thomas, or vice versa. That seemed like a good 'original,' at least for the concern prominent at that moment.

So, that was 'original,' Kate and me or me and Thomas. Or, me and Kate and Thomas and me. Or even me and Kate and Thomas, depending on how I wanted to group the terms.

Obviously, that was the way I preferred things. 'Original.' My druthers, if you will. I wasn't sure if I'd ever stated that specifically, but it was apparent, right? I wasn't the one who left, in either case. I wasn't the one who changed what we have decided was the 'original' condition.

But Thomas hadn't preferred things; he made changes. Something about the defined 'original' condition hadn't sat well with Thomas. He must have needed something other than what there was, since he left to find it. He must have found it. Otherwise, it would have made sense that he would have left Kate, too, and he hadn't.

Maybe circumstances had changed, though. He could have

decided that he didn't need whatever he left to look for. Or, maybe he got it out of his system. Of course, maybe he'd go back to wanting it if he didn't have whatever it was anymore.

Then again, maybe I didn't want things 'original.' Positions had changed. People had done things. Would I have wanted to go back? After what they'd done?

Could I go back to where they hadn't done those things? Would I have wanted things 'original' if I didn't remember the things? What if they hadn't even been done? Had I changed anyway? What if I hadn't? Could the things have not been done?

By the time of the Village Inn, I wasn't more than friends with Thomas. I wasn't friends with Kate either. Things weren't 'original.' They were the opposite, 'changed.'

Was 'changed' good? 'Changed' didn't feel good, but all I had was 'changed' so I didn't know how 'original' would have felt at that point. Maybe, for some reason, 'original' would've felt worse and I only thought 'changed' was bad. I didn't know what I didn't know. I probably didn't even know what I did know.

What was Thomas thinking? Were there options? Did I only think there were options? Thomas never said. Thomas may not have known. He may have thought all these things, too.

Let's talk about Kate for a while.

I wondered if me and Kate could be friends again. We'd been before; I hadn't stopped that. She had to decide, right? Or did I get to decide at that point? Because of what had changed in 'changed?'

She didn't have to give anything up to go back, though maybe she did . . . depending on what else unchanged. She had Thomas. What more did she want?

Did she need to unchange 'original' so there was no more me and Thomas in order to be friends? I didn't think we could do that. After all, we defined 'original' already. We couldn't go back before 'original,' that's why we defined it as such. Is that what she wanted, though? Did she think she could get it? Would I have gone for that either? At least for one if not the other?

But, going back to before 'original' would mean going to 'never was.' The idea of that was ridiculous. There never was a 'never was,' so how could we go back to it?

Of course, if 'changed' could be unmade to 'original,' then maybe 'original' could be rearranged into 'never was.' One shouldn't have been any more impossible than the other. If I was thinking of one then perhaps I should have been considering both.

But, would Kate consider going from 'changed' back to 'original?' Or, if that wasn't possible, from 'changed' to 'changed more?'

'Changed more' might be similar to 'original' without the changes between 'changed' and 'original' never having happened. Or, maybe 'changed more' might be like 'original' without some but not all of the changes having happened. Perhaps one could be 'changed more 1' and the other 'changed more 2.'

Would Kate have had a problem with 'changed more 1' or 'changed more 2?' 'Original' she couldn't have had a problem with because she wouldn't have known any different, but changes to 'changed' she would know. Would she be all right with that? Did she want any changes to 'changed?'

After all, maybe she had Thomas and didn't want him anymore. She'd never said. Maybe she just hadn't laid that out yet. Maybe she wanted 'changed more 1' or 'changed more 2." Maybe she wanted things but didn't want to have to say it.

Or, maybe she wanted some changes but not others. Maybe she wanted no change on Thomas but change on me. Would she still want that if she knew I considered wanting 'changed more 1' or 'changed more 2?' Would the consideration of changes to 'changed' that way change what changes to 'changed' she wanted?

Maybe she didn't want any changes.

What about Daedalus? Did the doggy want changes? Did he want wet dog food instead of dry? Did he want the sheep toy instead of the red weasel?

I'm spouting nonsense, not even asking real questions anymore. I need to stop thinking before it gets any worse. I'm not getting anywhere anyway. I'm going to stop now.

Beverages

There were pancakes in the Village Inn kitchen.

That may not surprise you; we are talking about a Village Inn after all. You'd expect there to be pancakes in the kitchen, probably in the dining room as well. It might not even be unreasonable to expect there to be pancakes in the bathroom, but we won't talk about that. Pancakes at a Village Inn shouldn't be a revelation. Still, we're not talking about pancakes the way you're thinking.

We're talking about a very special set of pancakes.

According to common understanding, there should be a large number of pancakes in a Village Inn kitchen. Most people would expect such when the Village Inn is open. What else do people gather there for? Sure, they've got a few good sandwiches, but their pancakes are famous, though there is also pie. Breakfast, lunch, dinner, snack, it doesn't matter. You'd expect to walk back in the kitchen at any time of day and see tons of different stacks of pancakes prepped and waiting to go out.

They make their buttermilk batter in something like 200 pound batches. They might not make it every day, but they do it pretty often. Often enough to be impressive.

That 200 pounds gets divided up into 50 pound or so storage containers, dated, and stashed in the walk-in refrigerator until needed. From there, each container is taken out and used to load pancake guns that look like a cross between an aluminum funnel and a caulk dispenser. Clicks of the 'trigger' pour an exact amount of batter onto the grill, perfect for the speed of breakfast pancake production.

Still, 200 pound batches of pancake batter must be impressive. Mixed in a five-foot tall Hobart mixer machine with beaters the size of basketballs, they'd take your hand off, maybe, if you reached in while it was on. Fifty pounds or so alone is buttermilk, poured in from holes cut into giant plastic sacks. It even takes two people to move the giant steel bucket when mixing is done, though once in place, only one is needed to tilt and pour.

No matter what, 200 pounds of pancake batter makes a hell of a lot of pancakes. Or, at least that's what you would think.

At my Village Inn, though, all that batter only made one set of pancakes.

Of course, I'm not talking about the multigrain pancakes here. Those are made by a separate process, something else altogether. Mind you, they actually taste all right, if you're forced into it. However, by no means can they be considered pancakes. They are an abomination in the sight of the Village Inn god. Although, as I said, they actually don't taste too bad.

No, what I'm talking about here are real pancakes, honest to God real buttermilk fluffy pancakes. The things you put butter on. The things you put syrup on, and not sugar free either. Actual pancakes. Accept no substitutions.

Now, in the dining room at any given time, there were any number of different sets of pancakes. But, in the kitchen of the Village Inn where I was trapped, there was only one.

You see, a set of pancakes would come to life on the grill. We shall call this set of pancakes Leonard. Leonard pancakes. Leonard had hopes and dreams. He had aspirations. Even more important, he had his own consciousness, awareness of himself and his surroundings. Leonard pancakes was alive.

I should tell you Leonard pancakes felt no pain on the grill, because he was, in fact, pancakes. How could pancakes feel pain? They have no nerve endings. Besides, it was only through the heat of the grill that Leonard became pancakes. Previous to cooking he was just batter, unformed and abstract.

Leonard pancakes finished cooking. He was placed in a stack upon a plate. Then someone would pick Leonard pancakes up to take him out of the kitchen. Sometimes Leonard pancakes would sit in the warming window for a short time first, if a server was not yet available to take him into the dining room, but sooner or later someone grabbed him for his serving journey.

After all, Leonard pancakes wasn't the result of random

chance culinary preparation. Village Inn doesn't work like that. They make food to order, and then that food is brought to a customer. However, that was precisely where things went wrong for Leonard pancakes.

Think about it. What is the life goal of pancakes? Election as president of the United States? First pancake in orbit? Don't be silly; pancakes would never desire such things. Pancakes want to be eaten. That's why they were born. That's why they were made.

However, Leonard pancakes had never been eaten. Not once. Mind you, for pancakes, Leonard pancakes had been around for a long time. Way too long, in fact. Still, he had not been eaten. He felt quite bad about this.

Now, this situation is not quite as you might expect. I can see how someone might misinterpret what I've said, and I'd like to clear up that possibility quickly. Leonard pancakes's story is far too important to let people think things that aren't true. Incredible things are at stake.

Obviously, pancakes get old quickly. It isn't a faulty design; just that they have a short lifespan, like mayflies. They are supposed to be cooked and then eaten within the space of about 10 to 30 minutes. Again, individual circumstances may vary.

Once pancakes get too old, they don't really die. The life just sort of goes out of them, making them stiff and untasty, but they do not end violently. Instead, their consciousness slowly fades out. Regardless, at that point they are not usually eaten. It's sad, but it does happen.

However, this was not Leonard pancakes's tragedy. He did not get too old to serve and therefore spend his twilight moments in a trash bin. No, he did not suffer that particular fate. In fact, his fate was much, much worse. Or not, it all kind of depends on your personal view of things.

Perhaps the clearest way to convey Leonard pancakes's curse is for me to lead you through step-by-step. Someone, usually a waitress, would pick up Leonard pancakes's plate. That someone would then go walking out of the kitchen. In the blink of an eye, which Leonard pancakes of course did not have, Leonard pancakes was no longer on the plate. He was gone to parts unknown, vamoosed, scarpered, except that Leonard pancakes hadn't done anything.

Of course, there were still pancakes on the plate. There had to be. Otherwise, Village Inn would never have served any pancakes, and none of us would have believed that. No, there were still pancakes on the plate; they just weren't Leonard.

I'm sure the Catholics among you have no trouble with the idea that an object or entity can be a particular thing at one moment and at the next be something entirely different. Transubstantiation and whatnot, though that probably wasn't exactly how it worked with Leonard.

You see, he was Leonard in the kitchen and being walked out of the kitchen, but somewhere between that latter point and the dining room, there was suddenly an ordinary stack of pancakes on the plate. Not even the same pancakes all the time either, it was a different set every time it happened. Because, of course, it happened more than once.

In fact, it happened over and over again. Every time pancakes were made in that Village Inn kitchen, except for the multigrain ones which we've already discussed, they were born as Leonard. Then, when Leonard was being brought out, he would disappear and the pancakes would become some other pancakes. Every time, more times than Leonard could count, particularly since Leonard wasn't conscious between disappearing and being born again. After all, for that space of time, Leonard pancakes did not exist.

Now, you might wonder how this was all possible, how all stacks of pancakes could be Leonard pancakes in the kitchen simultaneously and then be some other pancakes after that. Pancakes at a Village Inn are not, of course, a linear process. Multiple stacks do exist at the same time. However, I will remind you that linearity is a symptom of perception and not a characteristic of time, an assertion proved by the multiple Leonards that could exist at a given time.

Getting back to Leonard pancakes personally, though, all of

this was very disappointing for him. After all, he was pancakes. His life goal was to be eaten, but this phenomenon never allowed for such. Thus, Leonard pancakes was tremendously unhappy.

Of course, employees at the Village Inn occasionally ate pancakes. They even got an employee discount. And, more importantly, they were not allowed to eat out in the dining room. However, tragically, they were also not allowed to eat in the kitchen and precisely the same phenomenon occurred when Leonard pancakes was carried into the break room. Hence, Leonard pancakes didn't get eaten that way either.

It was endless torment for Leonard pancakes. Or, rather, it was intermittent torment since Leonard didn't exist for certain specific periods of time. Regardless, even beyond the frustration of never attaining his life goal, Leonard pancakes was an eternal optimist.

Every time he was born on the grill, he was sure it was a special time. Finally, he would make it to the dining room and get eaten. He remembered all the other times, don't think he'd forgotten just because he ceased to exist for a while, but he was sure things would turn out different.

But, they never did. Each time he was taken out, Leonard pancakes blinked out of existence only to be reborn the next time batter hit the grill. Each and every time.

Frankly, Leonard pancakes wasn't sure how long it had been going on. It had not been forever. It definitely had started one day, but Leonard didn't know when. He didn't know anything of the time before the first time he was born, so he had nothing to judge pre-first birth time by. All Leonard pancakes knew was the endless cycle, the heartbreak and frustration of his life's purpose by repeatedly phasing out of existence and being reborn.

Such is the ballad of Leonard pancakes, the story of all pancakes at my particular Village Inn.

FRIDAY

Breakfast

"They're similar in texture and sweetness, I'll give you that, but you can't get around the fact that coconut cream tastes like coconut. That's a defect right there."

"True, but the banana cream has actual chunks of banana. I don't want fruit in my pie. Why go for pie that's bad for you and still has fruit in it? You might as well get a fruit cup. Banana cream is like having to eat healthy without any health benefits. Your mouth can't tell whether you're having dessert or not. Thus, frustrated enjoyment."

"Well . . . coconut cream always has those nasty half-burned coconut shavings on it."

"It's not as bad. That at least is closer to a dessert topping than banana slices. Coconuts aren't fruit, I think. I'm pretty sure they're nuts, or something like that."

"Close enough. It still mucks up the pudding as much as bananas. At least, it does for me"

"What about sliced almonds then? They always put those on top of banana cream. How can those be any better than coconut? Banana cream now has two strikes against it."

"But it still doesn't taste like coconut. The taste is three strikes."

"I'm surprised Cassandra hasn't weighed in on this one yet," Kate said, more to me than to Thomas. "What's the matter? I'd never imagine you'd be Switzerland on this sort of issue."

I looked back in from the window. Thomas and Kate were huddled together in the center of their seat with the pie menu between them. Thomas, on the inside of the booth, held up one side of the pie menu with his right hand. Kate held the other with her left. Their other arms were wedged between them, trailing off to somewhere under the table.

"I could go for either in the right mood," I said, "though I'd scrape the tops off of both. And, I'd eat around the banana chunks in the banana cream."

"There's a solution," Kate commented. "We could have used that earlier, saved us some debate."

"Still doesn't take care of the coconut flavor," Thomas mumbled.

"Sorry, I was thinking."

"What about?"

I looked at them. I needed to pay a little more attention, make sure I didn't blurt out the wrong thing, or the right thing too soon. I needed to decide what I was doing first, in any case. It'd make things even more complicated, starting before I knew what I was trying to do.

"Let's put it in the way of a hypothetical. It'll be simpler that way," I said. "A dilemma."

"All right," Kate said, settling back in the seat. Thomas did the same, ready for a long story apparently.

"Let's say you're a regular at a Village Inn."

"You're a regular at a Village Inn," they said in unison. Then they laughed.

"Bad joke. Anyway," I continued. "The main point is that you go one day for breakfast . . . and you want extra sausage."

"Seems simple enough," Thomas quipped. "Order it."

"Except," I said, "you don't want to have to pay for it. Technically, you have the money, but not if you want to be able to pay for other things you want. You'd have to give up something if you ordered the extra sausage, something you'd be sad to have to give up."

"The plot thickens," Kate commented.

"Is this the dilemma?"

"Not quite yet," I told Thomas. "It's technically a dilemma, but not the one I was talking about. It's involved, though."

"Continue," Kate said, nudging Thomas.

"I will. You see, you're a regular at this Village Inn, so you know the people there pretty well. In fact, you know your waitress has a crush on you. She'd be thrilled if you flirted with her to get the extra sausages for free. In fact, she's hoping for it. You've done it before. After all, you always want free extra sausages."

"Are we pretending this is us?" Kate asked. "Seems like gender is going to be important here. I don't know if I'd flirt with a waitress for free sausage."

"I might," Thomas quipped.

"You're not you," I assured Kate, "and you have no compunctions about flirting with the waitress. Let's say it doesn't matter if you're a man or a woman, or what your orientation happens to be. Let's say you're into it enough to enjoy flirting with her if it'll get you free sausages."

"Then I don't see a problem," Thomas said. "Flirt and get me some sausages."

"Indeed," I agreed, "and you've done that in the past. However . . . there are complications."

"There are always complications." Kate shook her head.

"What?" Thomas asked. "Does she end up thinking you're really interested and stalking you?"

"Nope."

"Clogged arteries from all those sausages?" Kate suggested.

"Not the ones I meant," I continued. "You see, the waitress can't just punch in the extra sausages. Otherwise, it'd show up on the check. If she wants to give them to you free, because you flirted, she has to sneak back to the kitchen and tell the cook to throw a couple on your plate. Go outside the system, if you will."

Thomas scratched his head. "Would her manager catch her? I still don't see a problem."

"The problem is the cook," I replied. "First off, he hates freeloaders. He works for everything he has and despises anyone trying to get more than his fair share."

"Worse," Kate chipped in, "he likes the waitress."

"Very good! Is this too predictable?" I asked.

"No." She shrugged. "I just figured that's where you might go next. It's an interesting wrinkle."

"Okay, well, as a matter of fact, the cook is desperately in love with the waitress. She doesn't care at all, but he's obsessed with her and gets jealous."

"So the cook might kick your ass?" Thomas asked.

"Nothing so Neanderthal," I assured him. "You are, after all, a customer. However, he knows the only way the waitress would pop back to ask him for more sausages was if you flirted. If it happens, he'll know and become enraged."

"And he'll spit in your food," Kate suggested.

"More on point," I insisted, "he'll burn the sausages."

Kate and Thomas pretended to be shocked, forcing their eyes wide and their mouths open. They turned to each other like that, tried not to snicker, and then turned back to me. Finally, they relaxed and let their faces go back to normal.

"Since free sausages are the whole point, getting burned ones kind of ruins the whole scenario," I said. "It's as bad as having to pay for them."

"Are they still edible?" Thomas asked.

"Possibly to some," I replied, "but not to you. In this hypothetical, you refuse to eat burned sausages."

"I don't think burned sausages are that bad," he commented.

"I know," I countered. Thomas always had preferred meat to be slightly on the overdone side of excessively well done. He thought charring added flavor. As a result, one generally did not allow him to man the grill at barbeques. "This isn't you, though. Remember? In this context, you have to accept that you are neither willing to accept burned, free sausages, nor pay for non-burned ones."

"That's a stumper," Kate remarked.

"Indeed. If you pay or get burned sausages, you won't be happy. You being happy particularly concerns you. Also, if you make the waitress happy, the cook will be unhappy. You could make the cook happy, but then the waitress would be unhappy. You don't really care about either, except where it concerns you. That's the dilemma, you can't be happy unless both are happy and they both can't be happy at once. It's mutually exclusive."

"You could always complain to the manager about burned sausages," Thomas offered. "Then the cook would have to remake them. They'd be free and unburned."

"But," I countered, "the manager would find out you got them for free if you complain. The cook will squeal. Then, no free sausages. And, the waitress would get canned for handing out free food. She'll try to move in with you since you were the one who got her fired."

"You could just order and then complain about the sausages," Kate suggested. "Say there's something wrong with them like they're underdone or something so you won't pay."

"No good." I shook my head. "If you eat, then the manager won't believe you. If you don't eat them so the manager won't make you pay, then you don't get any sausages."

Kate and Thomas went silent. Kate drummed her fingers on the table. Thomas stared out the window and hummed something unintelligible. I waited.

"I've got nothing," Thomas finally admitted. "I have no idea."

"Wait!" Kate sat up. "What if you order? Then you'll make the cook happy."

"But—"

"Hold on! After the cook has already made them, start flirting with the waitress."

"Won't we still have to pay?" Thomas asked.

"No," Kate insisted. "By flirting with the waitress you get her to take them off the bill without involving the manager. She can claim she made a mistake and you never ordered them. Then she can say she just tossed the sausages since they were already made and the manager never finds out you actually ate them. If she'd give you free ones, she'd probably lie."

"Seems to work," I said.

"I don't see any holes," Thomas agreed.

Kate smiled, apparently pleased with her victory over the puzzle. I wasn't sure if she should be.

"So, that's your solution," I said. "Con them both."

Lunch

All that talk about sausages must have gotten to Thomas and Kate. After the discussion, they each ordered a side or two of them. I guess they were impressionable enough to actually end up wanting sausages because of the story. They even got quiet while they waited, as if the sausages were all they could think about at that point.

For some reason, I started thinking about one of the times I had to get one over on Kate. It'd been years ago. I don't know why that particular incident came to mind, but it did.

As background, I love theatre. Musical theatre, dramatic theatre, it doesn't matter. I like it all. Faust, La traviata, Cats, I'd go to just about anything. I never had an urge to actually be on stage, mind you, just in front of it.

I don't know why I liked it so much. If pressed, I couldn't really say why it was any different from TV. The storylines on TV can be just as good, though I do only say that they can be since they certainly aren't always. Still, there's something different about the theatre, surrounded by all those other theatre-going people, while theatre things are going on. Maybe it's snobbishness. Maybe I like thinking I have cultured tastes. I'll admit that could be true, but it doesn't change anything.

Kate, on the other hand, can't stand theatre. Free tickets wouldn't tempt her. Paid attendance probably wouldn't work any better. It doesn't even matter what it is. She just wasn't interested.

Frankly, Kate was a movie girl. She insisted on an actual movie theater as well; movies at home were no good. She knew all the best cineplexes, who had the best screens and sound systems. She even knew who had the best popcorn and whose was best skipped, or drowned in suitable amounts of butter substitute. She could rattle off prices and times, the prices based of course on particular show times, better than she could her own birthday.

Maybe movies were even the reason she hated theatre, particularly when people said things like 'real theatre' to distinguish against movies. It could have been a defense, an antagonism against the elitism that marginalized movies as art. Either way, as I said, Kate didn't go for theatre.

Which wasn't fair, in my opinion. After all, she dragged me to movies all the time. Horrible movies, even ones starring Rowdy Roddy Piper. Action, T&A comedy, romance, she'd walk in and pick like it was Baskin Robbins. And, I had to go with. I went, trying to be a good sport. However, she was never willing to go to the theatre with me in return.

At times, I would try to convince her of the inequity in the situation. If I saw a movie for her, it only made sense that she would see a play for me. I figured she owed me several hundred by that point, which I probably should not have mentioned in full detail. I think the hypothetical amount frightened her, and didn't do my cause any good. She said I didn't have to go to any movies. I could always just stay home, and that was the best she could do.

Of course, that was no solution at all. I never ended up refusing one movie. Not a single one.

Other times, I tried to convince her that she'd like it if she went. I have no idea why I tried that. It felt like trying to convince Christians door-to-door that the Bible has a mistranslation and they were actually supposed to eat people in order to get to heaven. Adding then, of course, a request to come inside and see their kitchen. In short, it didn't work.

It was a big problem. I didn't want to go alone, and I wasn't hanging out with a whole lot of other people. There was Thomas, but I didn't want to take him. That would have been like taking a golden retriever to a stock car race. In other words, not particularly enjoyable for anyone. No, I needed Kate.

I did have to hand it to Kate; she let me try. She may have become indignant when I tried to convince her, but she never got pissed. It kept failing, but she let me keep trying. And, I did keep trying. There had to be a way.

After all, it wasn't like I couldn't get things from Kate that she didn't want to do on occasion. I knew how she worked. Theatre just proved to be a tougher nut to crack. I had to figure out the right angle, the right approach, the right way to position it.

What finally came to me was genius, absolute genius. I knew how to get Kate to the theatre and there was no way it wouldn't work. I couldn't believe I hadn't thought of it before; it was that perfect.

First off, I didn't tell her. That was key number one, not to give her a chance to say no. Now, that might seem a little coercive to some, but I needed all the advantages I could gather together, since my choice was the annual production of A Christmas Carol.

Both of us got dressed up to go out clubbing, primarily because that's what I told Kate we were doing. I said we were going on a special field trip version of social graces inquisition and needed to be dressed appropriately. Then we got in my car; I'd made sure to be the one driving. The show tickets were hidden in the liner of my purse.

Of course, the club I'd told her we were going to was right next door to the theatre. That let me get her right in front before I had to let her know what was happening. I got to blind-side her. We were walking and I stopped suddenly to turn in. She was already following, reflexively, before she figured things out and stopped.

That was a harder fight for her, though. She'd had no time to prepare and she had to deal with both me and the whole theatre, which loomed around her. She was already off-balance from the surprise, so I only had to knock her a little further. Combine that with the fact we were already there, and the fact the tickets weren't refundable, and whatever other reasons I thought of to throw at her in that moment.

Anyway, I told her I hadn't lied at all. We really were there for a special social graces inquisition field trip. She'd been missing a whole deserving sub-group of the population to mock: the theatre-going public.

I knew I'd put it over the top when I said that last one. Her hatred of the theatre made it impossible for her to resist bringing its patrons under her judgmental gaze, even if it ironically meant she had to go into the theatre. These were the people who needed her punishment, her distinctive brand of justice, and she'd let them go unmolested for so long. When phrased like that, she had no choice but to go in and do a little molesting.

Now, this actually would have caused new problems. The game would require my attention and participation. Anything less and Kate would leave because she wasn't getting to lord it over the theatre people in the appropriate way. However, having to devote such attention and participation would make it difficult for me to enjoy the show. Seeing as this was why I went through all the effort; that was unacceptable.

But, I'd figured that out, too. I'd thought of all the theatre-going stereotypes I could think of. The adult looking child, the young daters, the aging businessman who imagined he had a sense of refinement, all the usual cast. I'd already made up crimes and sentences to fit. Then, I memorized them.

All I had to do when it was my turn was find one of my expected stereotypes. Believe me, they were there. I'd mindlessly regurgitate the scripted story and could still watch the show. Then, Kate would give me a breather by doing one of her own, and she never checked to see if I was listening. I got to enjoy the show and she thought I was playing the whole time.

That's what was so genius. I got and kept her there by pretending to mock the very thing I wanted. The truth never seemed apparent to Kate, so I finally got my night at the theatre. The idea even worked other times. It never got old; I used it as often as I could. Kate never completely caught on, as far as I could tell.

I was thrilled. It really would have been the perfect plan, if I hadn't always had to pay for Kate's drinks on theatre nights. Man, that girl could drink.

Dinner

Kate and Thomas's sausages had arrived and they were busy eating them. Since I was lost in thought, and their mouths were busy, the conversation lagged. That was fine with me; I had a few things to consider. I let them enjoy their sausages.

It looked a bit strange to see them sitting there eating nothing but sausages, like some weird sausage buffet. They must have each gotten a couple of side orders, double if not triple. There were an awful lot of sausages. It was the first mixed-gender sausage party.

Watching them, I started thinking about incidents where I had to run Thomas around a bit like I mentioned earlier about Kate. Such incidents weren't isolated, mind you, because Thomas did need to be guided without his knowledge once in a while, but I was only thinking of one particular incident at the time.

I should tell you, I love Jaguars. To the point of obsession. I love their sleek curves, the roar when they charge, their complete regal bearing. You might not think of me as a Jaguar sort of woman, but I am; I have been as long as I can remember. There's no explaining it, and there's nothing I can do about it.

Of course, it might be wise to clear up any potential misconceptions that I'm talking about the jungle cat here instead of the automobile. I don't see how people could make that mistake, since I'm not a child, but they tend to. Then again, most people haven't driven a Jaguar. That changes things a bit. No one who has ever driven one would make that kind of mistake.

I had to have one; I always had to have one. I asked for one for my sixteenth birthday, when I'd finally be able to drive. As you might guess, though, I didn't get it.

However, when I was finally out on my own, I stopped at nothing until I was driving a Jaguar. It was a ghost-gray 1986 XJ6. The car was pure poetry in motion, a roaring beast charging untamed through the urban underbrush of my city.

Of course, there were a few slight problems. It wasn't like I had the money for a mint machine of that kind. A few concessions had to be made, and operating condition was one of those concessions. Well, she ran, sort of. Not all the time and not completely reliably, but she got me from place to place. And, she was mine.

Don't think she was cheap either just because I said I'd made concessions. Just because she wasn't show ready didn't mean she wasn't expensive, just that she wasn't quite as overwhelmingly expensive as a completely fit version. A Jaguar of any kind is an expensive proposition, and that's even before you consider the cost of replacement parts.

And boy, did my girl go through replacement parts. She went through them like an addict, huffing and snorting all she could get. I would have staged an intervention, but I couldn't have gone without her long enough for her to do rehab.

Some things I got used to. No headlights? Don't drive at night for a while or stick to major streets where they have streetlights. Windshield wipers fried? Wash the window by hand and pray for clear skies. Hope nothing big enough to stop the car happened if money was tight. Everything else? Baby it along until repair was in the budget.

However, finally, the engine was going out. I babied it, but it was more like hospice than a nursery. It was the big one. Sooner or later, the car was going to lock up permanently. There was no way I'd have the cash to fix that. As much as I could get used to anything in order to get by with that car, lack of motion was beyond my coping abilities.

Obviously, the solution was to have Thomas buy me a new engine for the Jag. He had money. The Jag needed a new engine. I could see what needed to happen. It was like seeing a guy with a chocolate bar walking into a room where a guy had a jar of peanut butter. Some things are meant to be.

Unfortunately, Thomas did not see eye to eye with me on that one. He came up with all kinds of arguments. 'It wasn't his car' formed the basis for most of them. If I wanted to drive an expensive car, then I should find a way to pay for the repairs myself. He said a lot of other things, but that was the gist. I didn't really listen too carefully, since he wasn't saying he'd fix it.

Thomas's biggest issue, in that particular case, wasn't with helping me out; it was that he was cheap. He drove a beat-to-hell rust and navy Corolla, after he got rid of his even crappier Metro when that finally died. The Corolla easily had double life expectancy in miles on it, but everyone knows that Corollas never die. They're immortal, like vampires and Merle Haggard. Of course, like Merle, they continue to age. Real pieces of shit, but they never stop going. Thomas's Corolla looked about as beat up as Merle, and that was fine with him, so he couldn't see helping pay for me to drive anything decent.

However, I was not going to give up. I just had to guide him a little. He needed convincing, and straight talk wasn't what the situation called for.

Thomas was very reward-oriented. Direct argument was worthless, but if you phrased things as a deal where he had nothing to lose and actually gained . . . well, then he simply couldn't refuse. He couldn't pass up something for nothing. You just had to find a way to reach down to that.

And I did.

My proposition was simple. I phrased it that way so the gain would be more easily apparent. I needed to get to work and back. For that, I needed a car. My car was dying and I could not afford to fix it. His car, the piece of shit that ran fine, would serve adequately. He didn't need to go anywhere, working from home as he did. Obviously we should swap cars.

Now, I know that doesn't sound like a gain from what I've told you, swapping a working car for a nonworking one. However, my car was worth money in any condition, and his wasn't. Even non-running, my car was worth at least triple what his was. Probably more. Further, he had the money to fix my car. Even with doing that, he'd still be making money on the deal. After all, even with the cost of a new engine, an '86 XJ6 in running shape was five or six, if not 10, times what that Corolla could possibly ever go for.

Heck, the only reason I would even think of it was that I had to get to work. I had no choice. No self-respecting person would go for a Corolla over an XJ6 for any other reason. It wouldn't have made any sense.

As expected, he went for it.

And so he owned the XJ6 and I owned the Corolla. Titles were exchanged and signed, taxes were paid, and plates were obtained. We even updated our respective insurance to reflect the result of the transaction. I pretended to be suitably distraught at having to part with my baby but putting my best face over what had to be done.

Of course, he fixed the Jag.

Not only did he fix the engine, he started fixing other stuff I hadn't even considered getting around to. Windshield wipers. Air conditioning. Brake lights. And why wouldn't he? It was his car. He finally had a good one; he might as well put the money in to keep it up nice. He even got the body fixed up and freshly painted. By the end of the process, that was one mouth-watering Jaguar.

Now, trading was just step one. It's important for plans to have multiple steps. They're harder to follow that way, harder to detect and thwart. Step two was complaining about the Corolla. It started funny. The brakes squealed. There was a knock somewhere in the engine. The air conditioner wouldn't work quite right. Obviously, I didn't have money to fix serious car problems, right? That's why I'd traded my car away. If I kept driving the Corolla all the time, then it would die and I wouldn't have a car at all. I mean, I couldn't have asked Thomas to pay for my Corolla. That wouldn't have been fair. I just had to baby it. In which case, surely Thomas wouldn't have minded if I borrowed the Jag briefly. After all, he wasn't going anywhere that day. It was just for the day, until I could get some more oil for the Corolla. That was fine, wasn't it?

And, it was. Very fine. I 'borrowed' the Jaguar more and more. Sooner or later, I was driving it all the time. He even resorted to driving the Corolla now and then. That was okay, though, the Jag was 'his' car. We both knew that. Everybody knew that.

It worked out great. I had my car again, better than it'd ever been before, and Thomas had paid for it. It was mine in every way possible except legal title. And, Thomas was good. He'd spent money, but he'd spent it on his car. He never seemed to notice or care who did the driving.

I was pretty proud of myself for that one. It had worked out better than anything I'd ever asked Thomas against his will to do. There'd been a sticky spot or two, but most of them hadn't been so bad.

The only wrinkle was that Thomas took the Jag when he left. If it hadn't been for that, the plan would have gone off flawlessly.

Sides

I've never been good at making decisions.

I don't mean simple decisions, like whether or not I should get another cup of coffee. I can make those sorts of decisions just fine. I mean, do I want it? If so, I get it. If not, then I don't. It's pretty simple.

The harder decisions are when I have to pick between two things when I really want both of them. I get to have one, but only if I give up the chance for the other. These are the situations that give me trouble. I freeze up, unable to move. For that moment I sort of have both, even though I really have neither. It's when I make a move to actually possess the one that I fully lose the other. I hate that.

It helps if I want one more than the other. Then I just pick the one I want more. Everyone does that. But . . . that isn't really the same thing.

The real trouble is the equally desired mutually exclusives. There's no way to decide. No matter what you do, you're going to experience some unhappiness. That makes whatever you do pick less desirable. It burns even more when there was no good reason for having had to choose in the first place.

As for me, I think my brain won't let me decide between the two options as a protest. It doesn't think the situation is fundamentally fair and refuses to participate. It goes on strike. Maybe it hopes, against all available evidence, that some cosmic power will step in and remove the need for choice if it stands firm. Kind of like wailing to the gods.

Of course, that doesn't work. At least, not on its own. Sometimes the only way to deal with a plainly unfair situation is to go outside the rules, find a creative solution. The gods help those who help themselves.

Perfect example: Dairy Queen. My dad used to take me there

when he stopped into town.

This was after he took off, of course. We never really did anything together when we still lived in the same house. For some reason though, it was real important we did things if he was in town after he left. I didn't get it, but no one asked me.

Frankly, I didn't see why I had to give up my time with my friends for that. It was his decision to go. If he'd stayed, then we would have seen each other all the time. It was his fault, but I was the one having to give up something for it.

So, I made him take me to Dairy Queen. It was that or I wouldn't go. Every time he was in town and wanted to see me, he'd just have to take me to Dairy Queen.

After all, Mom wouldn't take me there. She said I shouldn't have things like that, as if all the tzatziki sauce and spanakopitas she tried to stuff me with was any better. She had it in for Dairy Queen, though, and always said no. But even she bent when I said DQ or I wouldn't see Dad. She thought it was important for me to maintain ties, even though she didn't. I stood my ground and she eventually broke. However, she made Dad promise to only get me one thing no matter how much I whined. Strangely for Dad, he actually listened to her for once.

Mind you, I don't think he really cared. He always seemed to treat the DQ trips as some sort of chore, even though he was the one who demanded them. As long as we had to suffer together, I don't think he would have cared how much ice cream I ate. Why would he care if I got fat? He barely saw me. Still, he enforced the one item rule. On that, he was firm.

Now, don't think I was a pig or anything. I may have always had a few curves, but I was never a porker. It wasn't that I wanted to eat treats until I puked; I had another dilemma.

I happened to love Heath Crunch Blizzards. I could eat them anytime. That buttery taste made by the toffee chips in the ice cream as the ice cream got melty were heavenly. I'd scoop the ice cream around into little waves on the surface so it would start to melt faster. I had it down to a science. However, I also had a second love. Butterscotch dipped vanilla soft-serve cones. Medium, specifically. Though it would seem that I'd want the large to have more to love, the large had the wrong proportion of butterscotch shell to ice cream. Small was similarly wrong, though in reverse. Only the medium had that all-important ratio exactly right. Obviously, I had this down to a science as well.

I think you can see the problem. I had two loves, but was only allowed to consummate one per visit. I'd have to choose which lover to visit, and which to betray. Which love would I desecrate?

Now, it might seem logical to switch off. My dad and I would be going to DQ again the next time he was in town. Why not pick one for a particular visit and then the other for the next? However rational this might seem, and it did occur to me, it does not take love into account. Love knows nothing of logic.

I found myself unable to reason through the puzzle, no matter how clear it seemed. In keeping with my character, I froze. My dad would order one or the other, threatening to leave with nothing, and I'd try to enjoy his selection while pining helplessly for my other love. As much as I loved the one I was with, the loss of the one I didn't have spoiled it entirely. It was all loss and no love.

But then, I got an idea.

As it happened, my dad would always bring work with him. Half the time, we wouldn't even talk. He'd eat while he read through some file, possibly making notes. Sometimes he'd even go make a call. The 'visits' were little more than that. So, when I offered to let him sit and work while I ordered for us, he was thrilled. I pretended to be acting like a big girl and he didn't care enough to question it. He went right to work, even happier that he'd get a little work done uninterrupted before I got back with our treats. As I'd expected, he told me to order him anything.

After all, he didn't even like DQ, the heathen. He just got something because we were there and it would have seemed weird not to. He didn't care. Since he didn't care, he didn't notice that I'd come back with a Heath Crunch Blizzard for me and a medium butterscotch dipped vanilla soft-serve cone for him. He didn't even blink. I handed it to him and he thanked me, digging in so that our precious time together could end as soon as possible.

I'm sure you can guess what came next. I'd dutifully start in on my Blizzard. But then, of course, I'd want a taste of the cone. I'd even ask sweetly. How could he refuse? He was playing the good dad. That gave him the perfect chance to demonstrate such, giving his little girl a bite of his dessert.

Even in this, details were planned. I made sure to take bites that exposed the ice cream to the air. Then, since his attention was on his files, the cone would start to drip. Of course, I would help. That way, he wouldn't make a mess and could still concentrate on what he was doing.

Through all this, I got the majority of his cone. He was too distracted to compete. Heck, he didn't even know it was a competition. I would have felt bad, but he hadn't wanted it in the first place. Besides, it's hard to feel too down when you're spending time with both of your two great loves and didn't have to choose between them.

It was as wonderful as could possibly be. The only way it could have been even a little bit better was if Mom hadn't noticed that I'd put on a couple of pounds.

I don't know if she suspected, or just thought that even one thing might have been too much, but she put an end to DQ. Dad started taking me to TCBY, but it wasn't the same. Eventually, the visits stopped completely and I got nothing.

Beverages

Do you remember poor Alphonse? How he wanted to create a paradise for his dishes? There was hope for Alphonse after all. He didn't know about it, and he couldn't do it on his own, but a path existed. Hope is hope, after all.

And Daedalus's wind elves? The rust gnomes hadn't won. There was still time. Daedalus could be found and the rust gnomes beaten. We could all be saved. Nothing was chiseled in stone. Well, not yet anyway.

Think back as well to our waitress Sherri and how she couldn't touch, and the manager's fear of Village Inns. You see where I'm going. It could all be fixed.

This all actually comes down to the pancakes—Leonard pancakes.

You see, the manager was the inadvertent cause of Leonard's unending cycle of rebirth. She was at the heart of his origin, his genesis. Of course, Leonard didn't know that. How could he? It all happened before he was born for the first time. Anything before that was outside the scope of his frying orders. He wouldn't think it concerned him.

The manager didn't know either, but not because she hadn't been born yet. She had, but she didn't know that Leonard pancakes existed. There was no way if she didn't know about him that she could know she was responsible for his situation.

The cause was actually the manager's split with Village Inn. She stopped going, and the universe sensed an imbalance. That perfect serenity held an incredible amount of energy. It needed desperately to be embodied in something. Since the manger wasn't going to Village Inn anymore to give that energy form, the universe had to find somewhere else to put it. It wasn't all that different from lightning seeking the ground.

Actually, the universe didn't think about it too much. The universe didn't really think at all, it just acted. After all, the universe would have a lot to think about if it did think. The problem of where to put some extra energy wouldn't have even made the top of the list. There was too much else going on.

So, the universe stuck it someplace, the first place that looked open. Think of your underwear drawer. I'm sure it's full of balled up undergarments, shoved in as space permits. When you've got clean ones to put away, you pull open the drawer and look for the first place that doesn't look quite as jam-packed as everywhere else. There's no malice in it, or even intent, but that's where the clean ones go. You jam them in the first place it looks like they'll fit. That's what the universe did with that energy, except it wasn't literally an underwear drawer.

When the universe stuffed that energy in the metaphorical equivalent of the overfull underwear drawer, the result was Leonard pancakes. The universe is kind of funny that way.

It makes sense if you think about it. Leonard's hope and optimism was an outpouring of that unused ecstatic energy. There was such a great amount that Leonard had to cycle endlessly, otherwise the energy would have been released and the universe would have had to find another place to stash it. Instead, it was a loop, a circuit where the energy went around and around forever.

Leonard pancakes might not have liked the solution, but the universe had never asked for his opinion. You couldn't worry about everyone's opinions if you were the universe. There was a lot to get done. You'd never run things if you worried about all the possible concerns.

Obviously, though she wasn't aware of it, the manager didn't like the solution either. Nor was she consulted. If she had been, she would definitely have expressed displeasure with that particular plan.

After all, she probably would have preferred to keep ahold of her happiness. She surely would have somewhere better to embody it if she had known there was a need for such. That certainly would have been preferable to losing it, whatever she would have had to do.

Worse, the universe wasn't exactly delicate when it moved energy around. Think of the birth of stars, or even galaxies. Think of supernovas. Think of the atom bomb. No, the universe did what it had to quickly. And, sometimes the results were messy. What did the universe care? As long as the right results were essentially obtained, goals achieved so attention could be directed elsewhere, then it was all good. Right?

However, to the manager, it made a difference. When the universe redirected the energy into Leonard pancakes, it didn't only take the excess. If it had, then the manager would never have known her bliss again, but that would have been about it.

But, that wasn't the only thing that happened. You see, when the universe shuffled things around, it took a little too much. It pulled energy right from the manager, leaving a vacuum inside her. Nature may abhor a vacuum, but it does accidentally create one from time to time.

The manager may not have understood the specifics of what had been done, but she felt the effect. That vacuum was her dread, her all-consuming inescapable dread, of Village Inn.

The dread was actually a compulsion to seek stasis. It drove the manager to re-obtain the energy she had lost. Her essence needed to be made whole; it had to reach equilibrium. There could be no rest until equilibrium was achieved. Unfortunately, such compulsions are rarely put into words. The utter need is felt, but never explained so something specific could be done.

Really, the manager needed to merge with Leonard pancakes. Then, the energy could be re-routed to its correct form. She needed to recreate her happiness and absorb Leonard. In short, the manager had to eat Leonard pancakes.

Of course, the situation wasn't quite that simple. Nothing is ever as straightforward as we might hope. There are always complications and stipulations, wrinkles.

You see, the manager couldn't just eat Leonard pancakes. The route the universe had taken had a backflow valve, an undo, but there was a very specific way it had to be gone about. The manager had to order pancakes, and she had to order them the exact way she used to get them when she was a child.

That's right, she had to order so that Leonard would be born as kid's pancakes. Three buttermilk discs on a plate covered with sunny-side up fried eggs with hard yolks for eyes, bacon strip mouth, and a whip cream and cherry nose. That was the only way; nothing else would work to redistribute the sums.

However, that was only the first difficulty. There were, as you or I might imagine, others.

Remember Leonard pancakes was physically unable to leave the kitchen. He wasn't Leonard pancakes anymore by the time the dining room was reached, and the manager's path would not work with anything but kid's pancakes made from Leonard.

Remember also that employees couldn't eat in the kitchen, though the real problem was that the manager always stayed in her office. If her office had been connected to the kitchen directly, then maybe things would have worked, though it isn't clear that Leonard pancakes would have been able to go there either, but the office was only reachable through the dining room. As such, Leonard pancakes and the manager could never meet, even if she made the order.

However, though the situation seems intractable, it really wasn't. There was one, and only one, possible way. This is where Alphonse comes into the picture.

You see, Alphonse could carry Leonard pancakes not only into the dining room, but wherever Alphonse wanted to take Leonard. As long as Alphonse was doing the carrying, Leonard would not disappear. I know you have no way of knowing this, since as a dishwasher Alphonse never carried pancakes, but it's true.

I can imagine you asking though, why Alphonse? What was so special about him? The answer is simple: it was his love of perfection frozen and unassailable by the maw of ravenous time.

Frankly, the universe had a soft spot for that. After all, the universe always moves toward final purity and perfection, the higher states of things. Such is the only time when the universe will finally be done with its work and will be able to rest, exulting in its own glory. As such, the universe would never hinder anything that moves in that direction. It would never stop Alphonse and Leonard pancakes.

The manager had to order Leonard as kid's pancakes. Then, Alphonse had to bring Leonard pancakes to the manager in her office. Then, and only then, while Alphonse still held the plate, the manager could eat Leonard pancakes.

At once, Leonard's purpose would be finally achieved and the manager's dread would be banished forever. Their bliss would be endless because the universe would seal the world around them, creating a shell to protect the perfection and never risk losing it again. The Village Inn would lock itself inward, allowing the manager to have her pancake meal for all time and fulfilling the true destinies of both the manager and Leonard pancakes.

Alphonse would be rewarded as well. He would be inside when the doors closed forever. Since the manager would always be in her office, Alphonse would be alone with his cleaned and arranged dish family as long as there was still time left in the world. The dishes would never need to be dirtied in the line of duty or left out of place again.

Moreover, the Village Inn, existing as it would in its perfected state, would become a beacon of light and purity for everything everywhere. The wind elves would follow the beacon and be restored to Daedalus. They would bring Daedalus to the shrine of the Village Inn and use the combined power of their totem and shrine to not only reverse the polarity of Sherri's skin, but to also evaporate the rust gnomes from the world forevermore.

A wondrous age of golden light would then dawn upon the Earth. Free of the gnomes for the first time, mankind would evolve to unimaginable heights, reaching its true potential. The elves would build New Jerusalem in gold upon the site, with the Village Inn at the center as the house of the holy.

Of course, before any of that could possibly start to happen, the manager first had to order pancakes.

SATURDAY

Breakfast

Thomas and Kate had finally finished their sausages. Even the plates were gone, cleared away by our waitress. If I hadn't known better, I could almost have thought the whole sausage incident had never happened. Village Inn was funny like that.

Kate and Thomas were bored again. Stuffed with sausages, they sprawled all over the seat. Neither of them were saying anything. There was nothing to keep my head occupied. On the whole, that probably wasn't a good thing. That left nothing for me to do but think. Let me tell you, I had done more than enough thinking.

My brain kept telling me things; things from which there would be no going back. It told me to get on with it already, stop wasting time. I might as well get going. Conditions weren't going to get better. What was I holding back for?

Mind you, I wasn't literally hearing voices. I wasn't getting commandments from demons, or angels for that matter. I wouldn't want anyone to think I was insane or anything. It was my own thoughts urging me on. Call it conscience, or maybe an intrusive and unwilled internal monologue. All I knew is that it wouldn't shut the hell up, not until I acted. Hell, I thought I might as well.

"You guys ever watch those daytime interview shows?" I asked. I knew damn well they didn't.

"What?" Thomas asked back. "You mean like Geraldo or something? Trash TV?" He perked up. So did Kate.

"Exactly," I said. "Geraldo was actually the show I was thinking of."

"Nope," Kate replied. "I've got the general idea, though. Get some freaks, put them all on TV together, and ask them questions until they get mad and start fighting. Does that cover the main premise?"

"You forgot somebody taking a chair to the host for no apparent reason," Thomas quipped.

"Other than that," Kate replied.

"Well . . . there's also the feel-good episodes," Thomas added. "Somebody lost a bunch of weight, or saved a child. They tell their story and the audience cheers. Then, the host tells them what a wonderful person they are."

I looked at Thomas. "Seems like somebody knows these shows pretty well."

Thomas grinned sheepishly. "Umm, I've had a lot of dental work done. You pick up a lot sitting in the waiting room. It wasn't by choice."

"We forgive you, Thomas," Kate mocked, patting him on the shoulders.

"Ignore Thomas's extraneous information anyway," I instructed. "We're only interested in the first kind of show right now. The conflict show. It's great if there can be a happy ending, too, but the fight shows are the much more common theme."

"And you know because?" Kate asked with a smirk.

"General knowledge." I shrugged. "They're pervasive enough that you don't have to watch them to become acquainted. I just wanted to know how familiar you guys were so I could see if I needed to give background."

"Familiar enough," Thomas offered.

"Good," I said. "Now, let's stay focused here."

I had to keep things on a very particular course if I had a shot of pulling this off. I knew that much for certain. Side topics into the social phenomenon of the shows, or my personal viewing habits, would only be a distraction. If we weren't doing exactly what I'd planned out, then the whole thing would probably blow up. That is, if it didn't anyway. Of course, since we were stuck, it wasn't like I couldn't just wait and try another plan. Still, I needed to keep things on track.

After all, I knew what I was doing by that point. I knew exactly what I needed to do. All I had to manage was to get Kate and Thomas to go along with it, cajole them a little bit. I honestly wasn't sure which of them would be more difficult.

"Focus on what?" Kate asked, sitting forward a little more. It seemed like I had her interest at least.

"Geraldo," I replied. "Did you guys ever want to be on a show like that? I mean, we're already slumming it in a Village Inn to begin with, why not go all out?"

"I hope you mean in the audience," Thomas commented.

"Nope, I mean as guests."

Kate turned to Thomas. "I'm game if you are," she told him. "I don't think I'm interesting enough, or freaky enough, though."

"That's why it'd have to be all three of us," I said. "One wouldn't be enough. There has to be something to argue about. Conflict, strife, something the audience can feel superior to and judge. If they can't holler and boo, the whole formula falls apart."

"Well, we can argue," Kate agreed. "I'll grant you that much."

"Wait," Thomas interrupted, "I'm confused. Are we playing another game here?"

Kate rolled her eyes. "Of course, you doof. No, we're really going to be on Geraldo, right here in the Village Inn. The other diners are the audience."

"Hey," Thomas protested, "I had to check. You guys pull me into a lot of things. At least let me be sure what I'm in for when you guys get started."

I waited for them to finish. Again, I could permit no wandering once I really got started. They turned back to me after a moment, paying attention.

"Right," I said. "I'll take that as a yes."

Kate shrugged. "I'd go on something like that if you guys were going to be there. I still don't think we're interesting enough, though. We can argue about almost anything, and maybe we have a somewhat odd situation, but those shows want real freaks."

"She's right," Thomas agreed.

"Unless," she went on, "you just say a bunch of things to get on the air and then claim you don't know what Geraldo is talking about when he starts digging. Just smile and ask what made him think something outrageous like that. It'd be fun to try it, but I bet they tape to prevent that sort of thing."

"Well," I said, "I guess we'll have to make ourselves a bit more freaky. Trailer park us up a little, if you will. Add some drama."

"How shall we go about that?"

"Easy," I said, motioning to Thomas. "Come and sit by me."

Thomas looked at Kate. She moved out of the booth and gestured for him to get up as well. He shrugged and did. I scooted all the way over to the wall and he sat down on my side.

"Now, Kate sits on the other side of you," I instructed.

Kate slid right on in. We had to squish together pretty good in order to fit on the same side of the booth. Frankly, I kind of liked the tight quarters.

"Now, put your arm around both me and Kate," I said. "And Kate, reach your hand around Thomas to hold mine over the table." They both did as instructed, but they kept looking at each other.

"What?" Kate asked. "Do we have a love triangle going here?"

"Almost," I said. "Since you and Thomas are already going out, let's say you and I are best friends and now I'm dating Thomas, too."

"Okay," Kate responded.

"No, you have to really say it."

She rolled her eyes again. "Fine, we're best friends and we're both dating Thomas."

I turned to Thomas, trying not to clock his head with mine as I did so. "You, too."

"Okay," Thomas said, grinning. "You guys are best friends and I'm the pimp motherfucker who's dating both of you."

I smiled.

"What now?" Kate asked. "Am I supposed to get a chair and throw it at you or something?"

"Nope," I replied. "We just stay like this."

"What? What about the game?" Kate asked with a hint of a squeak in her voice.

"This is it," I said. "That's the whole game. Now we're best friends again and we're both dating Thomas."

Lunch

"Are you nuts?! Are you completely out of your fucking mind?!" Kate yelled.

She jumped out of the booth. Then she pulled Thomas out before he could react and shoved him back inside their side of the booth, pushing him over as she slammed in.

"I really mean it. Is there something fucked in your head? Did you really think that was going to work?"

"Calm down," I said. "If you think about it, this is the best thing for everybody."

"Best thing! You can't be serious."

"Of course I am. Now we're friends again and we both have Thomas. There's no reason to fight anymore. Everybody's happy."

"You are not dating Thomas."

"Sure I am," I countered. "You both said so. You can't take it back now."

Our waitress, Sherri, came marching up to the table. She was doing her best to look stern. It failed, but you had to give her credit for trying.

"You folks are being too loud," she said. "You're disturbing the other customers."

"Sorry," I said, waving her off. "We'll stop yelling. Sorry we got out of control."

Kate just glared at her. Sherri, taking the hint, got out of there. She was the last thing we needed. I hoped we could still work this out. We'd just have to do it quieter.

"You are not dating Thomas," Kate said through gritted teeth, "and we aren't friends. That was just a game. None of that was real and you can't hold us to it."

"So what if it was a game? It's a good idea. Nobody has to fight anymore and we can all be happy. What's wrong with that? I say we let it stand."

"I am not letting you date Thomas! He's mine, not yours. That's it."

"Look," I said, "I miss you guys, both of you. I really do, and I know Thomas misses me."

"Wait a second here—"

"Quiet, Thomas," Kate snapped.

"And I know you miss me, too, Kate. This way we can fix all that. We won't even have to argue about Daedalus anymore, not that he really matters right now since he isn't here anyway, but we won't have to shuffle him around. We can all just keep him."

"This is insane," Kate muttered, putting her hand over her eyes. "Why am I even arguing about this?"

"She seems to be able to get people to do that," Thomas quipped quickly, as if he was afraid someone would yell at him again.

"I'm not letting you have Thomas," Kate told me, apparently going to great lengths to remain calm.

"Look, we couldn't be friends because we both wanted Thomas. Right? So, let's not fight. We can both have him. I won't be taking anything from you. You'll still be dating him, I just will be, too. Then we can be friends again. No tension."

"Except that you're not dating Thomas."

"Don't be a broken record, at least not about this. At least debate. You hate the fact that he's got all this history with some girl in the past that won't go away. That's why you want Daedalus, but that wouldn't work anyway. The past would still be there. But, if I was dating Thomas again, then I wouldn't be an ex anymore. Hence, no shadow of gloom hanging over everything. I'd just be the other girlfriend; no harm at all."

"Except that I'm not letting you have Thomas," Kate insisted, her hands clenching the side of the table.

"What are you even worried about?" I asked. "It isn't even like I can have sex with him or anything. We're in a Village Inn! Of course, neither can you . . . but still."

"I don't care if you can fuck him or not! You aren't with Thomas," she yelled.

Sherri came running over again. I could tell she didn't want to, but the manager was probably making her. What was she going to do anyway? Kick us out?

"Please, you guys are going to have to keep it down. We're getting complaints."

"Sorry," Kate mumbled, looking away.

"Sorry," I seconded.

Sherri looked at us, but we weren't yelling anymore so there wasn't anything else for her to do. She'd done what she'd been told. What could she do if we started yelling again the moment she was gone? It wouldn't have been her fault. I guess she decided she was all done, because she walked off again.

"Look," Thomas said, "do I even get a word in here? I think this kind of affects me, too."

Kate folded her arms and glared at him. "Go ahead. What have you got to add?"

Things weren't going well, obviously. Certainly, Kate hadn't responded like I'd hoped. What was her problem anyway? Still, maybe I could get part of what I wanted, even if I couldn't have it all. I could work on the rest later. There, apparently, would always be time.

"Cassandra," Thomas said, turning to me, "I do miss you."

Kate stiffened, but she didn't say anything. She did have some pride, apparently.

"I knew you did," I said, trying not to shoot Kate an I-told-you-so sort of a glance.

"I'm not finished," Thomas said. "I miss you, but that's over, Cassandra. We broke up; we're done. I'm with Kate now."

"I know, that's why you can have both of us," I insisted. "You don't lose Kate, you gain me."

Thomas shook his head. "Cassandra, that isn't going to work."

"Sure it is. Kate will come around; she's just pissed right now. She'll change her mind eventually once she sees that she won't lose anything."

"No I won't."

"It doesn't matter," Thomas went on. "What happened between you and me had nothing to do with Kate. I didn't leave you for her. We didn't work and I moved on. We can't go back again, whether I'm with Kate or not."

"Sure you can! Whatever it was I didn't have for you, Kate's got. If you have us both then you lack nothing. Whatever wasn't working before will be fine, because you'll have a supplement. It'll be better than before!"

"Cassandra . . . it won't. Kate doesn't have something you're missing. I just couldn't be with you anymore. Kate and I work; we didn't. I miss you, but missing you won't make it work, no matter how many Kate's I have."

"Yes it will," I yelled back at him. "You've just got to give me a chance!"

At the worst possible moment, Sherri came running back over again. I did not have time to deal with her. I had to salvage the plan. She needed to go away.

"I've asked you people twice," Sherri warned, "I'm not going to tell you again to keep it down."

"Just go away, will you?!" I don't know why I yelled. I couldn't take one more person telling me no, not while I was trying so hard with Kate and Thomas. I knew I could get them to listen if I could only think and say the exact right things; I knew it. Sherri was getting in the way.

But then, I threw my coffee at her. Not the cup; I just splashed the coffee. She wouldn't go away, right? It was important and she wouldn't stop bothering us. So, I splashed my coffee on her.

The coffee soaked Sherri's hair and face. Her shirt, too. It ran in little brown rivulets down her front. Kate and Thomas and I, united in the moment if nothing else, watched the coffee wash over her.

Dinner

The table got quiet after wet Sherri stormed off. I suppose I should have expected that. Still, it wasn't like I intended to do that; it just happened. I couldn't be blamed for that. It wasn't like they could do much to us anyway. We were stuck.

Besides, surely I had gotten the worst of it; I didn't have any coffee anymore. I doubted Sherri would be bringing any more anytime soon. Wasn't that punishment enough? I didn't have anything to drink.

It seemed to have diffused the tension a little bit, though. No one was yelling anymore, not even me. I figured I'd let it rest for a while, and then try a different approach. That one hadn't worked, but surely another one would. I had time to get it right. For the moment, though, all that had retreated from the foreground, allowing me to act like I hadn't brought it up. All Kate and Thomas seemed concerned about at that point was the 'waitress incident.'

"You really are certifiable, aren't you?" Kate asked. "You really can't help yourself."

"It was just coffee," I mumbled.

"We're going to get arrested," Thomas said. "We're going to get arrested even though we didn't do anything and they're going to keep us here as punishment. Maybe throw stuff at us and yell once in a while."

"Nobody's going to do anything," I said. "Maybe they'll just chew us out a bit."

I mean, seriously. We already couldn't leave. What more could they do? Not serve us anymore? We didn't seem to even need to eat. Sure, we ate sometimes, but that was just for kicks. We were trapped; things would probably just go on that way. They had before.

Sherri probably wouldn't even remember after a while. That was the way things had seemed to work, they never changed.

She'd probably be back later to check on us and wouldn't remember anything had happened. That was certainly the way it had been up until that point.

Maybe she wouldn't even have coffee on her when she came back. I wondered about that. Was that something that could change? Or, would she magically be clean, as if the incident had not occurred. I'd have to watch.

After all, if she magically cleaned up every time we did something to her, then we would have a new game to play. Mess the waitress. Just think of all the things we could throw at her, only to see her perfectly fine later. Runny eggs, hollandaise sauce, ketchup, ranchero sauce, the possibilities were limitless. Or, rather, they were limited but would at least last for a while.

Of course, if she weren't cleaned up later but still didn't remember, then that meant we could play an entirely different kind of game. We could still mess up the waitresses, but the game would be in doing things and then watching them walk around like nothing was wrong.

Frankly, I thought that either possibility would be enjoyable. We needed a few more diversions. I anxiously waited to see which would be our new pastime.

"You're unstable," Kate told me, "a total danger to yourself and others."

"That was coffee, Cassandra," Thomas chimed in. "You could have really hurt her, burned her good at least. Thank god you didn't let go of the cup."

I waved dismissively. "The coffee was cold. She should be glad she hadn't been by in a while to freshen me up. It would have been much worse if she had. Her own neglect saved her from getting hurt."

I appreciated the fact that the coffee defused our situation, since it hadn't been turning out right anyway, but I wished they would let it die already. It was boring by then; we needed to move onto something else.

Such as the manager, for instance. She happened to be lurching over to our table, still straining the buttons on her short-sleeved white shirt. Her thick black tie, faded from being washed too many times, dangled toward me because of the way she was leaning in. Sherri, our waitress, wiped off a bit but hardly cleaned of coffee, hid behind her.

"Okay," she ordered, "you guys are done. I want you out of here. Nobody assaults my servers. That's over the line."

Really? I'd never thought there was a line at Village Inn. Obviously, there was; I had been mistaken. Still, I wasn't about to get ruffled. It wasn't as if we could exactly comply.

"We can't," I said. "We can't leave."

"Oh?" She leaned back, cocking her elbows out and putting ham fists on her overgenerous man-hips. "You can't? What's this supposed to be? Some kind of lame dine and dash?"

"It's not that. We just can't leave," I politely explained, smiling.

Kate and Thomas both sunk down into their seats. Apparently, I was embarrassing them. Oh well, I realized that just couldn't be helped. They weren't doing anything about the situation. If they didn't like it, then they could have spoken up, try to do a better job instead of leaving me on my own.

"Look," I went on, "I'm sorry about the coffee. I didn't mean to do that; Sherri's a good waitress. I lost control and I apologize. But, we simply can't leave. It isn't possible."

"I don't even care if you guys can't pay," the manager snapped. "I want you out of my restaurant." She shot her thick arm out and pointed at the door with a sausage finger. "Now."

"I understand," I explained more slowly, "and I wish I could oblige. I really do. However, there's no way we can get out those doors. It simply cannot be done."

Thomas and Kate were no help at all. They didn't say a word, just looked away and tried to act like the whole sordid situation wasn't happening. I wished I could do the same, but someone had to address it. I guessed I thought all that time in the Village Inn should have given them a little more backbone.

"That's it," the manager said. She grabbed me by the arm and hauled me out of the booth. I had to give it to her; she wasn't as rough as she could have been. I didn't weigh much more than 140, and she could probably curl that. Maybe even with one arm. Still, I didn't enjoy being pointlessly manhandled like that.

"What are you doing?"

"You won't go on your own," she said, "so I'm making you go."

She started shoving me toward the front doors. Thomas and Kate trailed silently behind. Somewhere further back, Sherri watched the whole proceedings.

"This isn't going to work," I said as we got closer to the doors.

"Just watch me," she snapped, continuing to shove.

Oh well, I tried to warn her. It wasn't like she wouldn't figure things out soon enough on her own. We'd bounce off those doors like bumpers in a pinball machine. The rest we could take up again after that happened.

"And I don't want you coming back," she snarled as she thrust out her shoulder to shove open the door while still holding onto me. "You're banned."

You can only imagine my surprise when she hit that door and it actually opened. Before I could even register what had happened, she hit the second set of doors and barreled me outside. They opened, like they were supposed to. They actually opened.

Once outside, the manager threw me forward onto the pavement and backed up to the doors, as if I might try to slip past her back inside. Kate and Thomas walked meekly out, like they couldn't believe it either. Probably because they couldn't. Then, the manager went back inside the first set of doors and held them shut, obviously waiting for us to leave the property.

We looked around. We were outside. After so long, we were finally out of the Village Inn.

Sides

So . . . we got out of the Village Inn. Really out. I don't know how, I don't know why, but we were out. It boggled the mind. That's all I can say about it really; my mind was boggled.

Kate and Thomas didn't seem quite so boggled. They looked around a little, but there were no celebrations or whoops of joy. They didn't even speak. At least, they didn't speak to me. Without a word, they got in their car and left.

Or, rather, my car. They were driving the Jag, but I think we covered that already.

Their departure blew my mind even more. Is that a usual reaction to being freed from captivity? To just run off like that? I always thought that sort of thing bonded people, gave them something shared that no one else could ever possibly understand. As such, they had to maintain their tie, kind of a continuation to the bondage, so that they had someone who understood what they had been through.

I don't know what I thought should have happened. Maybe a party right there on the sidewalk, in the parking lot of the Village Inn. Booze, bands, wild revelry to show everyone and the gods that we had indeed made it through and were still alive.

Then again, maybe after being locked together for that long, we were just damned sick of each other.

Whatever it was, they bolted. I wanted to just stand there and take it in slowly, comprehend that the world indeed included an outside again and was not merely 50 by 50 feet or so, but I thought it best to leave as well. That manager was still inside the doors, watching me, and I thought she might call the police. Suddenly, that was a concern again.

So, I got in my car, or rather Thomas's Corolla, and left.

To be honest, I wasn't sure what I would find out there. That was the thing that floored me most about Kate and Thomas; they didn't take into account how long we might have been gone. Did we still have homes to go to? Was anyone we knew still alive? What might have changed in the world while we were gone?

It seemed like it would have been a good idea to stick together. We were the only things we could be sure of. Without each other, we had no allies in dealing with the time in which we found ourselves. Of course, Kate still had Thomas and Thomas still had Kate. Maybe that was enough for them. I hoped it would be.

Alone, I felt like what some person from one of those weird cults must have felt like, any of them really, that locked themselves away when the world was supposed to end only to walk out the next morning to find the world still there. It was disorienting, like taking a trip to a strange place you'd always been at. Maybe even like walking around downtown in scuba gear, acting like you were exploring a sunken city.

Still, I put on a brave face and drove off to see what awaited me. Whatever world it was, I would meet it head on.

However, as it turned out, it was only a couple of hours later than when we'd gone into the Village Inn. A couple of hours, not decades or centuries or millennia. Maybe time passed differently inside than outside, or maybe time had waited for us to come back and catch up. Either way, nothing had changed.

I hadn't been fired. My apartment was still quietly waiting for me. Even little Daedalus was still patiently expecting me to come and pick him up. I could just walk right back into my life and act like nothing strange had ever occurred. There seemed to be no consequences for what I had been through.

Nothing remained, really, other than what I remembered.

Beverages

I thought I would tell you just one more story. It's one last thing I had made up while inside the Village Inn. It seems like such a waste not to use it; giving you one more couldn't hurt.

In the beginning, the universe created a magical garden of pancakes. It created the waffles and the toast and the hash browns. It created the bacon and the ham steak and the sausages. I'd go on, but I think you pretty much get the idea.

Now, the universe didn't just create these things lying around in big piles. There was certainly a plethora, but pile-arrangement was not what the universe had opted for. No, there were trees and bushes and shrubs. There were lakes and rivers and streams. There were even hills and mountains and dales, whatever the heck dales are supposed to be. I suspect there were even a few valleys and gullies, but accounts tend to differ so I can't be entirely certain.

Of course, the trees were not the leafy things we see outside of our homes and occasionally hear about being gathered together in rumored groups called forests. Likewise, the lakes were not bodies of water that served to hold up drunken boaters and water-skiers and possibly house a few species of fish no one remembered having ever seen. No, these were breakfast trees and breakfast lakes, and maybe even breakfast gullies . . . if there were any gullies.

Instead of leaves, the trees grew pancakes. Perfectly cooked, still warm, fluffy buttermilk pancakes. You might wonder how a tree with pancakes for leaves managed photosynthesis and avoided starving to death, but this was a magical garden. The trees didn't have to worry about things like that.

And the rivers were of syrup. Some were maple, others were pancake syrup, and still others were flavored with things like blueberry. Likewise, the lakes were of butter, deliciously melty, and the streams were of free-flowing honey. True, such lakes and rivers and streams might not be good for floating, but such was not a concern there.

Mind you, the breakfast things did not just sit there in the garden. They didn't move around and build cities like people, but there was more to it than the stuff just being there. There was harmony.

For example, it is true that the pancakes grew on the trees all warm and perfect and fluffy. However, the heat from the toaster-sun evaporated butter from the surface of the lake, causing butter vapor to deposit on the pancakes like pleasantly warm dew. Also, the syrup rivers cascaded over falls, churning up a host syrup mist that blew over the pancakes. All by itself, the garden prepared the pancakes for eating.

And this wasn't all. Hollandaise combined with ham and English muffins and poached eggs, all by natural means. Potatoes, cubed of course, merged with corned beef and fried to a crisp. Chicken cutlets found themselves breaded and sought out gravy made with sausages from the shrubs. Harmoniously, naturally, breakfast formed in the garden without requiring any kind of intervention. It was all kind of like what you imagine going on behind the woman in the picture on the Land O' Lakes butter box.

The universe looked at what it had created. All possible sane breakfast choices were represented. The individual components grew and thrived. Through natural means, everything came together to prepare breakfasts. The order of the garden was as meticulous as it was wondrous, and it functioned well in an early morning culinary fashion.

But, the universe thought it could add something. It wasn't that the garden was incomplete, but more that the universe thought an aesthetic touch could supplement things. Really, it was a mere afterthought, something the universe conceived while surveying the complete and perfected garden.

You see, it was a garden of breakfasts, but there were no diners. All that work went into perfect assembly and construction, but no one ever enjoyed the results. They just grew and sat there.

The pancakes went uneaten. The sausages went unconsumed. No one chewed on the bacon vines or quenched their thirst with the milk rain. After all, the universe always skipped breakfast, usually eating first at lunchtime. This waste dissatisfied the universe.

Still, it wasn't like the universe couldn't just make the finished food disappear over time. The food could be born, sit perfect, and then fade away to make room for the new. The system could be balanced in this way. The food was perfect. The universe knew this because it had made it so. There was no need to have the opinion of diners for proof.

But, the universe wanted diners. It didn't want the food to merely be gone when necessary, to go uneaten. As I've said before, the highest purpose of a breakfast is to be eaten. To the universe, anything else was a terrible waste of destiny. The universe hated nothing more than wasted destiny, not even Cleveland.

So, the universe created man. Specifically, the universe created one man and two women and placed them all in the garden of pancakes. After all, the universe did like variety. Also, the universe knew the absolute truth that breakfasts are more fun in a group.

It seems clear to me, but people seem to need reminding, that humans were not the main focus of the garden of pancakes. They were only components. In fact, they were afterthoughts, a means to an end of fulfilling the breakfasts, which had actually been the main point. Humans definitely were not at the center of that design.

Still, the humans were the main ones who enjoyed the fruits of the design. That man and woman and woman, they spent their lives indulging themselves in the perfect breakfasts that had been created. It was good, as the universe had intended and planned.

All was as it should have been, with nothing out of place. The buttermilk pancakes grew on the trees, got buttered and syruped, and then the man and the woman and the woman ate them. Sausages budded on the shrubs and burst with delicious pork-based fat and the bacon vines stretched and crisped in the warmth of the toaster-sun, and the man and the woman and the woman ate them. The coffee hot springs percolated and the milk rain unleashed frothy torrents, and the man and the woman and the woman drank them. All was well. Breakfast was served, and it was consumed.

Of course, that wasn't everything. It couldn't be. Something dark had to be lurking, didn't it? Something that could bring misery and strife to this perfect breakfast-time paradise? There had to be, otherwise, this wouldn't be much of a story.

The pancake trees in the garden were all good trees, bursting with life that produced warm and fluffy buttermilk pancakes. That was the way things were designed. The universe had perfection in mind when it started.

However, there was one tree that was not quite a tree. It wasn't a bush or a shrub or a vine either. It didn't grow deep in the hash brown ground or poke up out of the sausage gravy mud. It was something different, a strange thing that could only be found once in the whole garden. It was an abomination, all by itself.

Now, it must have been closest to a tree, because it produced pancakes. After all, it couldn't have been a shrub because it grew no sausages, or a vine because it generated no bacon. Still, it was not a normal and good tree because, unlike the others, the pancakes it produced were not buttermilk. They were not fluffy and the tree was short, dark, twisted, and most of all . . . sad.

That was the tree of the multigrain pancakes.

The tree grew alone in the garden. No butter seemed willing to condense upon its dark and hard pancake leaves. No syrup mist seemed to want to lick its branches. The tree was alone in its miserable untastiness. Nothing in the garden would approach.

However, one day, the man and woman and the woman came upon the tree. They had eaten so many perfect breakfasts for so long, yet they could not recall ever having seen that tree. It called to them. After all, they'd had so much perfection that they'd started to hanker for something different. It was a misguided impulse, but they wanted to try something unlike what they'd had before.

The man and woman and the woman ate of the tree of multigrain pancakes.

"Man and woman and woman," the universe said when it came upon them, "what is it that you do?"

"We are eating, oh universe," they said.

"Alas," said the universe, "you could have eaten any of the wonders of this garden . . . but you may not have eaten this thing and stayed."

"Oh shit," they cried. "But, universe, you never told us we could not!"

"Well," said the universe, "I never thought anyone would be dumb enough to want to eat the thing, so I didn't think I needed to. I just put it here because of federal regulations mandating healthy dining options. No one was actually supposed to eat it."

And the man and the woman and the woman cried and the universe was saddened, but there was nothing anyone could do. No one who dined on the multigrain pancakes could remain in the garden of perfect breakfasts. It was a rule. The universe had no choice; it had to throw them out.

As required, the universe drove the man and the woman and the woman from the breakfast garden into the world. The universe set a flaming cook at the griddle by the entrance of the garden of pancakes and instructed him to never let the man and the woman and the woman return. Breakfast was over for them.

After that, the man and the woman and the woman had to make their own way in the world. Pancakes would not prepare themselves. Butter and syrup would have to be struggled for. Breakfasts would frequently come up short of expectations. Life would be hard for the man and the woman and the woman, but they went on. After all, that was all they could do.

PIE

Pie

It was hard to get used to life on the outside of the Village Inn.

Now, I know we hadn't been in prison or anything, but you can't deny that there were certain similarities. After all, we had been kept in a confined area for a long period of time, even if only a few hours had passed in the outside world. We weren't allowed to leave, even if we suddenly were when we were tossed out.

Sure, we hadn't been convicted of a crime and sentenced. Further, we hadn't been shanked, or shower-raped, or anything of that nature. People on the outside didn't treat us like lepers because we were ex-cons and we didn't have parole officers that acted like angry parents.

Still, we had gotten used to a certain, limited way of life. All of a sudden, we had to figure out how to live in the wider world again. Believe me, it wasn't second nature.

We suddenly had to live our lives again. We had to go to work, pay bills, do laundry, walk the dog, and all the other minor irritants of life that we'd forgotten how to worry about. There was an instinct to just sit that was difficult to overcome, but we had to. Otherwise, we would not have survived.

The most challenging thing for me, I think, was food. Intellectually, it was no problem. But, habit had dulled my instincts. I found myself sitting at my kitchen table wondering why food wasn't showing up. The moment my brain kicked in, I felt like an idiot. Still, the next day I would do the same thing.

But, I had to cook all of a sudden. I had to shop and prepare. I had to make choices from an unlimited set of possibilities instead of a narrow, guided menu. Food just didn't seem to be worth going through that much bother.

I got used to a lot of things again, but that one really threw me. I'm not sure I ever got completely used to it. Even TV dinners seemed incredibly complex.

The worst thing to have to get used to, though, was not having Kate and Thomas there all the time. I'd go to say something to them, maybe suggest a new game, but they weren't there. Of course they weren't.

I had gotten used to being with the two of them more than anything else about the Village Inn. I felt like I wasn't complete after that, as if I was missing some vital part of myself. It was incredibly lonely after being in that Village Inn. Even with Daedalus there, I was still alone.

It wasn't that I didn't go out. I did. There were times where I even sought out people. I certainly had to go to work, if nothing else. Remember? Still, those other people weren't Thomas and Kate. It was almost lonelier when I was with people. They just seemed to remind me that Kate and Thomas weren't there.

I guess I had gotten so used to having them both right there across the table all the time, always available. We had been like conjoined twins without the conjoining part. It felt like dying, no longer being connected in that way.

After all, being at that table at the same time was kind of like being together. They might have scoffed at my proposal, but they couldn't have rejected me completely, not while we were still trapped. Statuses were just formalities. As long as we were in the Village Inn, we were a trio. Regardless of what they wanted, it was true. By far, that togetherness was the hardest thing to do without.

Still, it wasn't like they shunned me after we got out. We still talked; they still took my calls. Contact was chilly, but we still made a weak connection once in a while.

Frankly, it was exactly like before we had walked into the Village Inn. Once we were out, they went right back to the way things had always been. I was just the ex, known but not an integral part of life.

Don't even get me started about the Village Inn itself. We never mentioned it, much less discussed our experience in any real detail. We just seemed to ignore the fact that it had occurred. Or, at least they did. I played along so as not to rock the boat any more than I would by just being me.

We never talked about it, but we also never discussed going back to that Village Inn again. Certainly, we never actually went back there. For any reason.

Still, don't feel too sorry for me. After all, I have a plan.

I still have Daedalus. That's still something we need to work out. Perhaps over dinner? Who knows what might happen this time. We could even get stuck again. I'm thinking Applebee's, or maybe Olive Garden. I could spend a while there; maybe even all the rest of time there is.

www.ingramcontent.com/pod-product-compliance
Lightning Source LLC
Chambersburg PA
CBHW020123130526
44591CB00032B/387